Charles Grant

The Last Hundred Years of English Literature

Charles Grant

The Last Hundred Years of English Literature

ISBN/EAN: 9783337105990

Printed in Europe, USA, Canada, Australia, Japan

Cover: Foto ©ninafisch / pixelio.de

More available books at **www.hansebooks.com**

THE

LAST HUNDRED YEARS

OF

ENGLISH LITERATURE

BY

CHARLES GRANT.

JENA, FR. FROMMANN

LONDON, WILLIAMS AND NORGATE.

—

1866.

TO

MY MOTHER

I DEDICATE

THIS BOOK.

PREFACE.

This book is based on a course of lectures which I read in Jena in the winter of 1864—5. I then endeavoured to sketch the history of modern English literature by criticising the works of those poets and novelists who have exercised the greatest influence over it, and pointing out the nature and extent of that influence. I confined myself almost entirely to works of imagination and mentioned none that did not seem to have a permanent value. I now offer those lectures in a modified form to a larger public. Though a great part has been rewritten and the whole carefully revised, this volume still bears, I fear, too many traces of its origin.

In the first book I have not mentioned those writers who like Sterne belonged in character to the preceeding period but confined my attention to those who prepared the way for the age of Wordsworth, Byron and Scott. In the last I have left unnoticed those who had not obtained a wide celebrity before the year 1860, though the later works of earlier writers will be found mentioned in the proper place. This rule which I have been obliged for many obvious reasons to observe has prevented me mentioning several interesting and remarkable works, as for example the dramas of Mr Swinburne, several novels of George Meredith and Henry Kingsley, the Angle House and many others.

The American literature did not seem to me to belong to my subject, for though it has doubtless been greatly influenced by that of England, and has in its turn exercised a great influence on that of the latter country, it has been modified by different circumstances, and is the result of a different form of social and national life.

The distance of any English library has rendered it impossible for me to verify my quotations from Robert Browning and Owen Meredith.

CONTENTS.

BOOK I.

1760 — 1·800.

Grant litterature.

CHAPTER I.

The poetry of the age that succeeded the Restoration differed widely from all that had gone before it. The revolution had passed like a deluge over England, and had obliterated the old landmarks. The traditions of the great age had been lost amid the storms of the civil wars. The whole character of English life had been changed. The courtiers who surrounded Charles II bore little or no resemblance to the Cavaliers who had fought round his father, still less did his subjects resemble the yeomanry who had gathered round "Good Queen Bess" in the hour of England's need. The theatres had been closed for years, and the masterpieces of the Eliszabethan drama were all but forgotten when they were reopened. Hence there was no English taste to oppose that which the courtiers imported from France. In their exile they had become acquainted with the literature of that country, and had imbibed its taste. To this the decline of our poetry has often been ascribed, and it doubtless hastened, though I do not think it caused it. It injured our poetry for the same reason that it stimulated our science, it brought us into connexion with the other nations of Europe, and so exposed us to the influences that were governing them.

The end of the seventeenth, and the beginning of the eighteenth century was the age of science as opposed to poetry. Everywhere in Europe there was an endeavour to systematize. Every thing must be weighed and measured

1 *

and explained. Human nature itself was reduced by the philosophers of the day to a mere system of forces. Man was to these thinkers nothing but a cunningly made machine. His moral nature was but a nicely adjusted balance, in which different interests were weighed. All that is demonic in our nature, the noble passion that makes men forget selfinterest, the fine enthusiasm that leads to self-abnegation, was either ignored, or put aside as folly and madness. In such a system there could be but small room for art. It could not, it is true, like religion be quite done away with, for the saloons must be decorated, and the philosophers must be amused, but it was degraded into a mere servant of luxury. A taste for music or pictures and a taste for wine were placed on nearly the same level, both were signs of an expensive education. Poetry was a little better treated than her sister arts. She was changed into a pedagogue. There were certain moral lessons which it was necessary to teach, and poetry was charged with the care of putting them into an agreeable form. As soon as she was safely installed in the school-room, a series of school-laws were drawn up according to which she was to teach. By these laws all poets living and dead were judged. Those who had written on other principles were misrepresented or condemned. The sublime poetry of Greece was cut down to the saloon standard; the luxurient and romantic literature of Spain was accused of fancifulness and childishness, while Shakspeare was put aside as a barbarian, who had now and then chanced upon a lucky thought. Didactic poetry became the favourite form of verse. The tales and dramas that were still written were moulded on a conventional standard. Neither imagination nor passion were allowed full scope. The flowing rhetoric of Dryden, and the polished brilliancy of Pope were prefered to the gorgeous imagination of Spenser, and the heartrending passion of Shakspeare. Nor was this dislike for the sublime and the irregular confined to art. Goldsmith preferred the scenery of the Netherlands to that of Scotland, and Addison wrote when at Geneva; — „My head is still giddy with mountains and precipices, and you can't imagine how much I am pleased with the sight of a plain, that is as agreeable to me at present as the sight of a shore was about a year ago, after our tempest at Genoa." These two poets were in many respects the representatives of their age. And Goldsmith at least had a much clearer perception of the beauties of nature than most of his contemporaries. Now a poet can hardly be expected to produce grand works of art when he is incapable of admiring the beauties of nature. Accordingly we find that the writers of this age paid more attention to their diction and rhythm than to any thing else. Even in this they were conventional. Neatness was considered the highest literary beauty, and the monotonous and stereotyped rhythmical forms of Pope were preferred to the wild melody of the poets of the Elizabethan age.

These faults must at least in part be attributed to the scientific spirit of the age. Literary criticism had become a science, but, like every other science, it was some time before it found the system it ought to persue. Indeed, before the time of Lessing, it bore almost the same resemblance to real criticism that alchymy does to chemistry. It was studied by many men of talent, and several truths were discovered. From these a few laws of more or less importance were deduced, but the system persued was false, and the end that was aimed at was impossible. Nor is this to be wondered at. Criticism presents more temptation to superficiality than any other science. A naturalist may ignore the phenomena which are opposed to his theory, but he cannot declare that nature is wrong in producing them or that they have no right to exist. A critic on the other hand can - and often must - say that works of great popularity are the results of a depraved taste. Thus he is at once discoverer, lawgiver, and judge.

How injurious the influence of the critics was, a single glance at the literature of this age will show. The value of each branch of it stands almost exactly in inverse proportion to their influence over it. Novel writing is almost the only department in which the century which succeeded the Restoration can be said to excel, and, in it, the influence of the critics was least felt. Yet even here it was all but insupportable, as the frequent and angry protests of Fielding and his contemporaries prove. If we turn to the Drama, we find that in tragedy where the laws were strictest, the age produced no single work that belongs to the first, and very few that stand high in the second class, while in comedy which, from its very nature, is more difficult to control, we find several names that belong to the very highest order. In satire it is true our rule does not hold good; but the laws that govern this style of writing are much more obvious than those of dramatical, epic or lyrical poetry, and they were well known to the critics of the day.

But not only were many of the rules which were at this time universally accepted superficial and injurious, the end they aimed at was unattainable, the foundation on which they rested was false. It was taken for granted that a standard could be fixed for every branch of literature. The writers of Germany, France, and England freed themselves as far as possible of their national typus, and endeavoured to approach this universal ideal as nearly as possible. Thus the drama of Greece was held up to universal admiration, and by it all plays were judged. The works of Shakspeare and Fletcher might be full of passion and humour, their characters might be drawn with exquisite truth, and their plots constructed with consummate skill, they had not observed the unities, and these beauties were as nothing in the balance, they were condemned. Now, if we compare the drama of Greece with that of England in the Elizabethan age, we find that each is perfect in its kind, and each is in some

respects superior to the other. In art, as in nature, there
are many kinds of beauty. Sophocles and Shakspeare were
both poets of the highest order, but a Shakspeare cut and
pruned into a bad imitation of Sophocles would be a monstrosity.

Still we cannot but confess that the critics of this age
conferred some very important benefits on our literature.
The drama of the Shakspearean age, with all its beauties,
was often barbarous, and the lyrical poetry of the same
period is frequently disfigured by quibbles and conceits.
Both these faults the critics of the French or classical school
banished from our poetry. Nor must we deny them the
credit of paving the way for a purer and more catholic taste
than their own.

Whatever the cause may have been, it cannot be
doubted that the poetry of England from the Restoration
down to the year 1760 or thereabouts was, taken as a
whole, very shallow and common-place. Swift is perhaps
the only writer of the period who had any thing gigantic
about him, and his was the grandeur of a fallen angel. For
the rest primness had usurped the place of beauty, and elegance that of grace. The same is true of France and Germany. Every where we find mental activity and scientific
research, nowhere any great creative power, or even a
capability of appreciating the sublimest works of art. In
that age there were people in England who thought that
Pope's translation of Homer was superior to the original, and
critics in France who preferred Racine to Sophocles. But,
after all, this false and artificial taste was confined to the
higher classes, it never became general among the people.
While Dryden and Addison were praised by the critics,
Shakspeare and Fletcher retained their places on the stage.
While the „Rape of the Lock" and the „Henriade" were admired by the fine gentlemen and ladies of Berlin and London, German peasants repeated, by the chimney corner, the

marvellous fairy tales which had been the delight of their
forefathers, and the wives of Scotch fishermen sung their
children to sleep with ballads whose passion and tenderness
will bear a comparison with any part of our literature.

In the year 1760 Dr. *Johnson*, *Oliver Goldsmith*, and
Lawrence Sterne were the greatest representatives of English
literature.   They were all men of talent, and even the se-
verest critic cannot deny genius to Sterne.   But in character
they belonged to the age that was passing away, so that we
cannot enter into an examination of their works.   For the
same reason we shall pass the plays of *Sheridan* without notice.   But about this time a reaction began in our poetry.
We may notice two circumstances which probably hastened,
though they did not cause it, and which were at least signs
that it was near.   *Garrick* had acted Shakspeare's plays to
admiring crowds, and Dr. Johnson's edition of the same poet
had been sold with extraordinary haste.   We cannot but
think that the crowds that thronged the theatre and the
students who read Lear and Macbeth in their studies could
not help asking themselves whence came the strange charm
of his writings, and why it was wanting in Cato, and the
other masterpieces which the classical school held up to their
admiration.   Be this as it may, a taste for our old literature,
and a longing for novelty grew up side by side.   The Poems
of Ossian were a very successful attempt to satisfy both.   The
popularity which this work once enjoyed all over Europe
renders it necessary for us to linger a few moments over it.

In the year 1760, *James Macpherson* published a work
entitled „Fragments of ancient poetry translated from the
Gaelic or Erse languages".   This volume consisted of a series
of Fragments, written in a very bombast and mannerized
prose style.   These were, as he stated, literal translations
of songs which were sung in Gaelic by the natives of the
North of Scotland, and were the works of a poet who lived,
probably, in the second or third century after Christ.   It

was not the first time that Macpherson had appeared before the public as an author. In his twenty first year he had published an heroic poem, „The Highlander", one of the worst of the miserable productions of that age. It had been treated with well deserved neglect. Another fate however awaited - his new volume. It attracted universal attention, and a subscription was made to enable him to travel through the Highlands and continue his studies. In 1762 he published „Fingal", an Epic poem in six books, and in 1763 „Temora" in eight books. These too he attributed to the same poet, *Ossian*. They caused one of the bitterest controversies which have raged in England. There can now be no doubt that they were forgeries, nor were they very ingenious forgeries; it is one of the greatest proofs of the shallowness of the age that they should ever have been considered genuine.

Let us turn for a moment to the real epics which have been handed down by word of mouth as these professed to be. The most remarkable of which we are possessed are the Iliad and the Odyssey, the Nibelungen and the Gudrunlied. Here we find the greatest simplicity. The poet has a tale to tell, and he tells it in the simplest manner. He is too busied with his subject to waste his time in seeking ornaments. He describes, when description is necessary to make us understand his tale, but never for the mere sake of describing, whereas the tale in Fingal is but a peg on which Ossian hangs gaudy and incorrect descriptions of nature, and other rags of tawdry finery. Again, in all really popular epics we find that, when pictures are used, they are used to make the sense clearer or more impressive, and not for their own sakes alone. In these poems, on the other hand, they are piled on each other till they obscure the sense and we see the characters moving, as it were, in a thick fog. In a narrative poem which is intended to be declaimed or sung, the interest must be centred on the story, and all minor beauties must be sacrificed, if they interfere with it.

Every thing must be clear and sharply drawn that it may
make the intended impression on the audience. This is the
case with all the works above mentioned. Let us take the
Nibelungenlied which approaches far more nearly than the
·Homeric poems the character of the age and nation to which
Ossian's works were attributed. Who that has read it ever
forgot a single incident in the tragic story? From the girlish
dream of Krimhilda to the death of the last of her race, each
scene lives as clearly in our memories as if we had seen the
whole. In Fingal, on the other hand, it is often difficult
to follow even the thread of the story, and but few could
retell even the outlines of the tale six weeks after reading
it through. In short, it has not one of the distinguishing
qualities of the class to which it was said to belong. But
this is not all. The Highland society, after making a strict
search, was unable to find any Gaelic poem which resembled
those of Macpherson. There can therefore, be no doubt that
the poems of Ossian were forgeries. Nor have they any
very great poetical value. But this only makes their popularity the more remarkable, as it is a proof of the desire
for novelty which was beginning to make itself felt in
England.

The next work which demands our attention is of a
very different kind. Dr. *Thomas Percy*, afterwards bishop
of Dromore, published in 1765 his „Reliques of Ancient ·
English poetry". This work was professedly based on a
manuscript of ancient ballads which had fallen into his
hands, but a great part consisted of lyrical poems from the
age of Elizabeth and Charles I. The older and rougher
pieces were smoothed and polished into something like modern rhythm, and, though critics and antiquarians may
blame him for this, we must confess that the poems exercised a much greater influence than they could otherwise
have done. These corrections, too, were made with so
much care, and the lyrical poems were chosen with so much

good taste, that it would be difficult to find a more delightful book in the whole range of our literature.

The English ballads contained in these volumes are, for the most part, the productions of the minstrels of the middle ages which had been handed down, by word of mouth, to comparatively modern times. That we do not possess them in their original form is clear from the variations of different copies. These changes were sometimes rendered necessary by the development of the language, by words and phrases growing obsolete and having to be replaced by new ones: oftener however they were the voluntary additions or alterations of the singer who looked upon the poem as a piece of property which he might treat as he liked. To this a great part of the life, force, and conciseness of expression which distinguish these poems seem to me to be owing. A clever declaimer would soon perceive which verses pleased, and which tired his audience, and he would be careful to retain the one, and leave out or alter the others. Again, on hearing a ballad in two forms, he would naturally choose the best verses of both versions. Thus, by a process not unlike that which is known in zoology as natural selection, a popular ballad would go on improving. Of course at a certain point of time this process would cease. When the minstrels had been superseded by books, and the old songs were no longer sung in the Baronial hall, or on the village green, they would become gradually corrupted and forgotten. A few old men would still remember the outlines of the story, but they would forget the incidents, and retain only a verse here and there till, at last, the ballads would sink with them into the silence of the grave. Thanks to Bishop Percy and the industrious collectors who followed him, we still possess a few in their most perfect form. We may divide them into two classes 1) those that treat historical events, and 2) those that treat subjects resembling those of our old romances. We have an excellent specimen of the first class in „Chevy Chase" and of the second in „Sir Cauline".

In the first of these poems the story is told as simply and straight forwardly as if it were written in prose. There is no ornament, nor is there any attempt to heighten the effect of the tale by the manner of telling it. The subject is grand and heroic, and the interest centres on the subject and not on the form. In these respects it bears no slight resemblance to the Nibelungenlied. In fact, though of course no one would think of comparing it with that incomparable poem, it belongs to the same class — to the poems that spring from the heart of a nation and therefore speak directly to every heart.

The ballads which treat romantic subjects differ, in many respects, from the above. If we compare „Sir Cauline" with the chivalrous romances, we find that it has much more simplicity, much more life, and a much greater dramatic power than they. Compared with the historical ballads, on the other hand, it seems highly ornamented, while the rhythm is much smother and more sonorous. The subject of the poem too is sentimental rather than heroic. It occupies, in short, a position between the romance and the ballad, and was doubtless a great favourite with all who had imbibed the spirit of chivalry.

The Scotch ballads contained in Percy's Reliques are, taken as a whole, far superior to those we have above examined. The subjects of the English poems are heroic and sentimental, these are tragic and pathetic. They were only stories, well and simply told, while these are full of bursts of wild and lyrical passion. Here too we have tales of war and battle, but they are no longer told by the merry and careless soldier or in his spirit, but by one whose heart has bled for those whom the hero has left behind him. They are filled with a strange wild pathos and tenderness. They treat a far larger range of feelings

than the English ballads. Patriotism, courage, and love are
almost the only feelings which the latter touch upon. They
delight in the glitter of the tournament and the pomp of
battle. The Scotch poets, on the other hand, prefer domestic crimes and incidents. They touch all our elementary
emotions by turn, from the lawless barbarous courage and
hate of the border ⚔ nobleman to the despair of a mother
weeping over her murdered children, from the wild joy of
battle to the agony of a vain remorse. „Edward“, whose
dark melancholy made such an impression on the mind of
Heine that he wove it into the unearthly plot of his youthful tragedy Radcliffe, is known to most Germans in Platen's
excellent, but rather too polished translation, but the following lines from „Edom o' Gordon“ seem to me even more
characteristic. That robber chieftain has set fire to the house
of his enemy during his absence, while his wife and children
are within.

> „O than bespaik [1] hir [2] little son,
>   Sate on the nurses knee:
> Says, „Mither [3] deare gi [4] owre [5] this house,
>   For the reek [6] it smithers [7] me.“
>
> „I wad [8] gie [4] a' [9] my gowd [10] my childe
>   Sae [11] wald [8] I a' my fee,
> For ane [12] blast o' [13] the western wind,
>   To blaw [14] the reck frae [15] thee.“
>
> O then bespaik hir dochter [16] dear,
>   She was baith [17] jimp [18] and sma [19]:
> „O row [20] me in a pair o' sheits [21],
>   And tow me owre the wa [23].“

---

1 spoke. 2 her. 3 mother. 4 give. 5 over, up. 6 smoke.
7 smothers. 8 would. 9 all. 10 gold. 11 so. 12 one. 13 of.
14 blow. 15 from. 16 daughter. 17 both. 18 slender. 19 small.
20 roll. 21 sheets. 23 wall.

They rowd hir in a pair o sheits,
    And towd hir owre the wa:
But on the point of Gordons spear
    She gat[24] a deadly fa.[25].

O bonnie[26] bonnie was hir mouth,
    And cherry were her cheiks[27],
And clear[28] clear was hir zellow[29] hair,
    Whereon the reid[30] bluid[31] dreips[32].

Then wi'[33] his spear he turnd hir owre,
    O gin[34] her face was wan!
He sayd[35], „Ze[36] are the first that eir[37]
    I wisht[38] alive again."

He turnd hir owre and owre againe,
    O gin[34] hir skin was whyte![39]
„I might ha[40] spared that bonnie face
    To hae[40] been sum[41] mans delyte[42].

Busk and boun[43], my merry men a',
    For ill dooms[44] I doe[45] guess,
I cannae[46] luik[47] in that bonnie face,
    As it lyes[48] on the grass."

The purely lyrical poems which Percy included in his
collection were either popular Scotch songs, or pieces chosen
from English poets who had already become antiquated. Most
of these belonged to the Elizabethan age, the greatest period
in the history of our literature. The lyrical poetry of that
time, it is true, is frequently disfigured by quibbles and conceits. It is often fanciful and sometimes artificial. Yet, in

---

24 got. 25 fall. 26 beautiful. 27 cheeks. 28 bright. 29 yellow.
30 red. 31 blood. 32 drips. 33 with. 34 a Scottish idiom to express great admiration. 35 said. 36 you. 37 ever. 38 wished.
39 white. 40 have. 41 some. 42 delight. 43 up and about.
44 fate. 45 do. 46 cannot. 47 look. 48 lies.

the purely lyrical element, in richness of imagery, in melody, and freshness of feeling the songs of that age are superior not only to all that the classical school produced, but to every thing our modern literature has to boast of, with the one exception of Burns' poems.

From the above it will at once be evident that *Percy's* „Reliques" was opposed, in almost every important respect, to the taste of the day. The beauties and the faults of the pieces contained in that work were the reverse of those which were in fashion at the time of its publication. The subjects in which the classical school had been most success- ful were didactic or satirical, the poems which formed the principal part of this collection were narrative or lyrical. The epigrammatic brilliancy, the studied elegance, and the artificial nicety of the followers of Pope were here brought into contrast with the barbarous grandeur, the wild imagi- nation, and the Titanic passion of the middle ages and the period which immediately succeeded them. They were not carefully weighed and polished verses, such as the critics then valued most highly, but they were the natural expres- sion of natural feelings. Hence the publication of this work marks the epoch in the history of our literature from which we may date the beginning of its reformation. We have lin- gered long over these volumes, but not longer than they deserve for they were at once the record of the past, and the herald of the future, the relics of the age which preceeded Shakespeare, and the text books of Bürger and Scott.

CHAPTER II.

Though Dr. Johnson and most of the other leading critics of the age were opposed to Percy's „Reliques" and treated it with great severity, it was on the whole well received by the public. This is a proof that a more healthy and Catholic taste than that of the classical school was gradually developing itself in England.

None felt this craving for a more imaginative and natural poetry more deeply than the talented and unfortunate *Thomas Chatterton*. He was born in Bristol on the 20ᵗʰ of November 1752. His father, who died before the birth of the poet, had been the teacher of the charity-school in that town, and all the education Chatterton ever had was picked up at a free school. Yet even under these unfavourable circumstances he exhibited a wonderful genius at an uncommonly early age.

At fourteen he was apprenticed to an attorney, in his native town, but he devoted much of his attention to poetry and antiquities. It is sad to think of a boy like Chatterton being bound down to the dreary and irksome routine of an attorneys office at so early an age. But his energy, his genius, and his untiring application surmounted every obstacle. His leisure time was spent in study or in wandering alone through the fields, and sketching the village churches near Bristol. Without a guide, a friend, or any one who could sympathize with his literary tastes, it is no wonder that the youthful poet should become excessively proud and sensitive. Yet these years were probably the happiest in his whole life, though even then we find that the thought of suicide was familiar to him. Young as he was, he was already busied with the great work of his life, a series of the most extraordinary literary forgeries in our language. He pretended to have discovered a number of ancient manuscripts, in an old box

which had been removed from Bristol Church as old lumber
by his grandfather, who had been sexton there. Most
of these manuscripts, the poet said, had been used by his
father as covers for school books, but some that remained
were works of the greatest interest. He published the first
in 1768 when he was but 16 years old. It was an account
of the opening of the old bridge at Bristol, taken, as he said,
from an ancient manuscript. After this he presented various
extracts from these writings to his friends, some in translations, and some in old English. At last he published a
series of poems in the Town and Country Magazine which
were written, as he said, by a Mr Canynge, and Thomas Rowley a priest in the 15th Century. These poems which were
written in old English occasioned a warm controversy among
literary antiquarians.

In April 1770 Chatterton was forced to leave his office.
Encouraged by his success in Bristol, he went to London
where he tried to support himself by writing for the book-
sellers. At first he seems to have been successful, as he
wrote very happy and hopeful letters to his mother and
sister, and even sent them several presents. He looked at
the essays and poems he wrote at this time merely as a
means of earning his bread, without taking any great interest
in the subjects he wrote upon. England, at that time,
was engaged in a great struggle, the court with the liberal
party; Chatterton alone, living in the midst of the struggle,
and writing continually about it, seems to have taken no
deep interest in public questions. „He is but a poor
author," he writes home, „who cannot write on both sides."
This is of course very wrong, but let us pause before we
condemn him. Let us remember how sad his life had been,
how his glorious genius had been cramped and fettered by
poverty, how manfully he was struggling for life, alone and
unaided in the midst of the busy battling world. Let us
remember, too, the tenderness of his letters to his mother,

and those little presents he sent her with his hardly earned
money. Nor must we forget how foreign all these questions
were to the great purposes and ends of his life. How could
the young poet, absorbed in what has been called the sublime egotism of Genius, be expected to take any great interest in political questions? How shall we dare to blame
the unhappy youth for laxity in respect of them? But papers, and poems written in such a frame of mind, and on
such subjects, cannot be expected to be of any great value.
Some of Chattertons were terse and well expressed, but this
is almost all that can be said in their praise. Thought and
opinion must become passion, before they become fit subjects for lyrical poems. This is not the case with these.

Literary employment, always proverbially uncertain,
was, at that period, more than usually so, and for a number
of reasons, which we have not time to enumerate, Chatterton got out of employment and sunk into real want. We
have not time to trace the misfortunes and vain struggles of
the ill fated youth. At last he was without a penny to buy
bread. Too proud to be a burden to his mother, or to ask
help of his friends, too wearied out and broken spirited
to make a last effort, he poisoned himself on the 25th of
August 1770. He was then seventeen years and nine
months old. „No English poet,“ says Campbell, „ever
equaled him at so early an age.“

The great work of Chatterton's life was the forgeries
of which I have spoken. They were collected and published
shortly after his death, under the title of „Poems, supposed
to have been written at Bristol, by Thomas Rowley and
others, in the fifteenth century.“ They are written in the
language, and mostly in the taste of that age. Here we
cannot but ask, what could have induced the youthful poet
to bind his genius by the use of crabbed and antiquated
dialect, and the imperfectly developed rhythmical forms
of that period? This question leads us to one of the most

wonderful characteristics of these poems — their thorough
objectiveness. Byron, whose sorrows, great as they doubtless were, cannot be compared with those of Chatterton,
spent his whole life in telling the world the doleful story of
his misfortunes. His genius modulated the notes, and added
depth and variety of colouring to the tale, but it could not
raise him above his woe. This comfort Chatterton scorned.
If we were to read the poems of Rowley without knowing
anything of their author, we should fancy he was sóme rich,
or at least some independent man, who was endowed with
an exquisite sense of beauty and melody, but had never
known much of sorrow: we should never imagine that he
was a poor, neglected and all but hopeless youth, who,
after battling bravely and even madly with the troubles of
the world, could find no place of rest but a grave. Chatterton, as we have seen, scorned the comfort which most
poets seem to find in such sympathy as they can beg from
their hearers, but he doubtless found a deeper and nobler
consolation in poetry. The world around him was dark and
dreary, his life was monotonous, and he was tired of its
drudgery, so he created an ideal world into which these
sorrows could never come. Into it he retired when the office was shut, and the days work over, and in it he met
the loving faces and kind hearts, that he sought in vain in
this. I must confess that, in excluding all the petty cares
and troubles of his every day life from his verses, he seems
to me to have acted better and more nobly, than those who
show their wounds, and boast of their sorrows. It is easy
to see why he laid the scene of his poem in such a distant
age. It was not only the pomp of chivalry, and the dreamy
retirement of monastic life which attracted him as they afterwards did the romantic school. Then our poetry had been
very different from the monotonous verses which the classical school had made the standard of excellence. The imperfectly developed forms of that period seemed sweeter to

2 *

his ear than the cold alexandrines of Pope, and the wild
luxuriance of fancy, in which our ancient poets delighted,
could not fail to attract an imagination so lively and vivid
as his. As to the old spelling, there is something strangely attractive in old words and forms of expression to those
who have pored long on old black letter volumes, and these
had been the chief intellectual food within Chattertons reach.
Besides, they were a necessary part of the forgery, if we
must call it by so hard a name, which he had determined to
carry out. Had he published his verses in his own name,
they would probably, even had he found a publisher, have
been cast aside unread as barbarous. But the poems of
Rowley, a monk of the 15th century, could not be treated
in so unceremonious a manner, nor could their author be
charged with barbarism for writing according to the tastes
of his age. But was the imitation successful? On this question much has been written and said and I think that lately
the skill of Chatterton has been rather under-than overvalued. It has often been said that Rowley's poems resemble
those of the poets of the first half of the nineteenth century,
rather than those of the fifteenth. But we must remember
that most of these poets imitated, either directly or in-
directly, our ancient literature, and the very parts of their
poems which resemble Chatterton's most are those which are
most like our pre-Elizabethan writers. There are, of
course, thoughts and lines in these poems which could not
have been written at the period to which their author
ascribed them. Such for instance is the criticism in the
epistle to Canynge:

> „Plays made from holy tales I hold unmeet;
>   Let some great story of a man be sung;
>   When, as a man, we God and Jesus treat,
>   In my poor mind, we do the Godhead wrong.“

It is not however by separate lines that such a work must

be judged, and, taken as a whole, the poet has been wonderfully successful.

We cannot now enter into a criticism of each of the
poems, they differ from each other very widely in value,
but taken as a whole, no one can deny that they prove that
their author possessed a highly refined taste, and considerable
genius. We cannot wonder that his contemporaries could not
believe him to be their author, for, from beginning to end,
there is nothing boyish in them. In the whole volume there
is no bombast, no false sentiment, sickly pathos, nor over-
drawn heroism. Can the same be said of the writings of
any other poet before reaching his eighteenth year? Who can
say what Chatterton might have become? We will not try
to guess. He stands as it is alone, the greatest English poet
of his own age, the only boy whose poems will last as long
as our language endures.

Yet his verses are not entirely free from faults. We
find in them the besetting sins of our pre-Elizabethan and
modern poetry. Chatterton, when once determined to palm
off his poems as ancient, could not, it is true, have avoided
them, but they are faults nevertheless. The greatest of
those is an inclination to use imagery for its own sake. This
is a fault into which the lyrical poets of the fourteenth, fifteenth, and sixteenth centuries frequently fell. It is also a
fault of some of our modern poets. This we often meet in
the writings of Chatterton, but it is so inextricably inter-
woven with many beauties that, while regretting its presence, we hardly know how the poet could have avoided it,
without destroying much we would not willingly lose. The
following lines will show what I mean:

Brown as the filbert dropping from the shell,
Brown as the nappy ale at Hochtide game,
So brown the crooked rings that featly fell
Over the neck of the all beauteous dame. —

       *   *
          *

Taper as candles laid at Cuthbert's shrine,
Taper as elms that Goodrickes abbey shrove,
Taper as silver chalices for wine,
So taper was her arms and shape yegrove⁄⁄.
As skillful miners by the stones above
Can know what metal is yelach'd below,
So Kennewalcha's face, yemade for love,
The lovely image of her soul did show;
Thus was she outward formed; the sun her mind
Did gild her mortal shape and all her charms refined.

It is quite clear that the „filberts", the „nappy ale",
the „candles", the „elms", and the „silver chalices" were
not used here to give a clearer idea of the lady whom the
poet is describing, but because they in themselves pleased
his fancy. It is just as clear too that this description
leaves no vivid impression on our minds. The pictures do
not place Kennewalcha before us, they rather draw our attention away from her. Yet we cannot deny that these
verses have a great beauty of their own. They recall lovely
scenes whose beauty the harshest critic must acknowledge.
I might mention the half philosophical lines in Ella as deficient in poetical feeling, but they are written so exactly in
the spirit of our earlier poets, and the local colouring is
so exquisitely worked out, that I incline to consider them
rather as a beauty than a defect. The weakest piece, in my
opinion, in the book is the much praised „Death of Sir
Charles Bawdin". It is written in imitation of our old ballad style, but the subject and manner were too far removed
from the circle of Chatterton's thoughts and feelings to be
successfully treated by him. Such were the great faults of
his verses, and surely it is rather a cause of wonder that
they are so few, than that these few are there. Living in
the midst of a prosaic and critic — ridden age, his poems
are remarkable for their freshness and force of imagination.
Their indirect effect on our literature has been all but in-

calculable. From him Wordsworth, Coleridge and Shelley learned much, and each of them has lamented his fate and celebrated his genius in verses of admirable tenderness and power. That he is little known out of England, and even there comparatively little read, is probably owing to the antiquated dialect in which his poems are written, which is much more difficult than the language of Chaucer and Gower. Such was the life, and such are the poems of Chatterton. Surely the sternest moralist will rather lament his untimely fate, than blame

The marvellous boy,
The sleepless soul that perished in his pride

for his last rash act. His poems will never cease to delight all lovers of the imaginative, but somewhat fanciful poetry of the middle ages. Nor will his name ever be mentioned without a sigh of regret, that one so gifted should have been so unfortunate, that so great a genius should not have survived to enjoy the fame he so well merited, and to leave behind him some great work, which might have taken its place among the noblest productions of our literature.

It would be difficult to find a character which presents a more thorough contrast to Chatterton in every respect than the man whose name stands next on our list — *William Cowper*. The one, born in the midst of poverty, and hemmed in with difficulties on every side, allowed none of these to mar, or even to colour his poems. The other, born of one of the highest English families, and in his whole life suffering scarcely any trouble that deserved the name, fretted himself into madness over imaginary evils. The one, urged on by the wild fire of Genius, was engaged during the greater part of his short life in a hopeless struggle with fate; the other, living retired from the world and far from its toil and turmoil, argued himself into despair by fears of an eternal punishment. Yet the works of William Cowper form an important link in the history of our lite-

rature. He was and perhaps still is the most popular poet
of his age. But he is most popular in circles where the
grandest productions of our literature are seldom read.

Cowper's mind was more nearly related to the classical
writers than to the great poets who preceeded them. His
favorite subjects are either didactic or satiric. He is seldom
passionate and enthusiastic. He is a dreamer rather than a
singer, and his dreams are not glorious visions of beauty
and of splendour, like those of Shelley, they are the reveries
and meditations of a religious recluse, who loves to linger
by the willowy streams, and to stray down the woodland
ways of English scenery. Yet his works did almost as much
to reform our literature as those we have been examining.

The classical poetry had become, as we have seen, almost inane, a series of polished lines without life, passion,
beauty, truth, or power. Percy and Chatterton had com-
bated this taste by republishing and reproducing our ancient
poetry. They had held up the simple truth and heroism of
our old ballads, and the wild imagination and tenderness of
ancient lyric to the admiration of the public. Cowper attacked the false taste of the day on another side — by the
studied truth of his details. He clothed the simple events
of every day in verse. He loved to tell his readers how well
Mrs Unwin made tea, and how they chatted over it, to talk
about his dogs and his hares, his walks and his day dreams.
Such subjects are not very grand or poetical, nor are his
verses brilliant, but his poetry is true. Nature breathes
through every line. This is the reason why he attained popularity, and still remains popular.

He was, however, most successful as a religious poet.
His hymns are among the best in our language, though they
have not the deep fervour of those of Wesley and Newton.
They are still sung in the churches and chapels of most English sects, and they deserve their popularity. They have,
it is true, many faults; the chief of which is that they are

often dogmatic, and the narrow creed of their author often spoils even the finest passages.

Percy, Chatterton and Cowper may be looked upon as the leaders of the literary revolution which dethroned the classical poets. They exercised a far greater influence over the taste of the succeeding age than any of their contemporaries. Indeed, we shall find that each of them may be looked upon as the forerunner of a particular school. We must pass over the minor poets of the age without notice, that we may have time for the Scotch literature of this period.

CHAPTER III.

The Scotch literature, during the latter half of the eighteenth century, differed very widely from that of England during the same period. It could not but be so. Down to 1707 England and Scotland had been different nations, governed, it is true, by the same sovereign, but in every other respect dissimilar to each other. The history of Scotland had been the story of a brave and succesful resistance to the unjust demands of her powerful neighbour. Nor was the history forgotten. It lived in the hearts of the people. Tales about Bruce and Wallace were still told by every fireside. Songs relating their deeds, and praising their bravery still passed from mouth to mouth. Nor did the union at first do much to diminish this feeling. The Scotch were treated by the English as a set of poor and greedy adventurers, who wished to prey on the riches of England, while they, in their turn, regarded the English as arrogant enemies who had managed to trick Scotland out of her freedom. Scotch too was not a dialect of English in the same sense as the languages of Suffolk and Yorkshire were dialects. It had, as its historians proudly and with truth asserted, a

thoroughly independent literature. Nor was this literature
contemptible. In the fifteenth century it had been one of
the finest in Europe. It was rich in Romances, fabliaux,
and satires. In short, the nations were, at the commencement of the last century, so thoroughly estranged that a
union with France would probably have been much more
popular in Scotland than that with England. Such was the
state of public feeling, when in 1745 Charles Edward landed
almost unattended in Scotland, and half the nation rallied
round its banished prince. The history of the rebellion does
not of course concern us at present, but the feeling that produced it is embodied in a series of songs which we cannot
leave unnoticed. In a political point of view the Jacobite
rebellion of 45 was foolish in the extreme, but looking at
it in a poetical light, by means of these songs, it would be
difficult to find a grander movement in modern history. The
story of the rebellion, even when simply and prosaically related, seems more like a wild chivalrous romance than a
piece of sober history. Charles Edward is well fitted to be
the hero of such a tale. Young, noble, brave, and hand-
some, the descendant of a long line of kings, he returned
from exile almost unattended, and quite unannounced. He
did not come to take the lead in a well organised insurrection, he came to win back, with his own hand, the crown
of his fathers, trusting to himself and the loyalty and bravery of his country alone. It is no wonder that the brave
and chivalrous highlanders rallied round him, that the low-
landers flocked to his standard, and that the poets of Scotland vied with each other in singing his praise. In their
eyes the Jacobite cause united every noble and disinterested
feeling. It was Scotland rising upon her old foes, who had
tricked and insulted her. It was a country rushing to welcome and defend the king that had been torn from her. It
was the old noblesse demanding vengeance on the men who
had pawned

The Scottish crown
To a wee bit German lairdie.
The prince was passionately welcomed, and his courage
proudly contrasted with George's phlegm in such songs as
this

Silken beds, and carpet rooms
Wad hardly do to suit Geordie,
Bot a far better prince, he lay on the groun',
Weel row'd up in his tarten plaidie.

Then came the bitter hour of woe and disappointment. The
Scotch army was defeated, its leaders imprisoned and executed, and the prince himself, the brave, the noble, the
heroic prince was flying from cottage to cottage, seeking in
vain a means of escape. Yet even then, Scotland, sung the
poets, had a right to be proud. While hiding among the
poorest free peasantry in Europe, known to almost every
one, no one was found to betray his king for the immense
sum the government had set upon his head. Then came the
songs of mingled joy and sorrow:

Bonnie Charlie's gane awa
Safely o'er the friendly main,
Mony a heart wad break in twa',
Should he niver come again.
Will ye nae come back again?
Will ye nae come back again?
Better lo'ed ye canna be.
Will ye nae come back again?

In short, almost every shade of feeling is mirrored in these
poems: hope, joy, exultation, sorrow, and despair. There
are playful poems, and poems that breathe a passionate affection and loyalty, that we cannot understand. Many of
them too are exquisitely beautiful, and will bear a comparison with the lyric poetry of any country in the world.
There were many causes for this rise in the Scotch lyric.
These songs were at once the death song of ancient Scotland,

with her chivalrous bravery, and the birth song of modern
Scotland, with her enterprise and industry; and, while the
philosopher and the politician go forth eagerly to meet the
new world, the poet and the artist cannot help casting a
longing lingering glance behind them „at the picturesque
ruins, and venerable abuses of the past." But Scotch poetry
did not die with Old Scotland. It sprung up, and blossomed,
and hung garlands and wreathes of ivy around the ruins
from which it sprung. We have seen that the old Scotch
ballads had been distinguished from those of England by
their melancholy, their tenderness, and the wild music of
their rhythm. These too were the characteristics of the
poems that succeeded them. But the subjects were changed.
It was no longer the border raid, or the highland foray
that was sung. The common events of every day modern
life, were now the burden of these songs. But they were
told by no retired recluse like Cowper, who sat musing by
the tea-urn, lost in the depths of philosophical contemplation.
They were sung by the men who had felt them, with tears .
or laughter, and sometimes with laughter mingled with
tears. The Scotch dialects are excellently suited for such
poetry. They are musical, forcible and expressive, and yet
they have something strangely simple about them, that reminds one of the prattling of a child.

No Scotch poet who immediately preceeded Burns
attained any great celebrity; yet the lyrical poetry of the
age as a whole is very rich. These songs are known by
many who never heard the name of their authors. They
have passed from mouth to mouth, and become the property
of the people. They are sung in the cottages of the highlands, and in the drawing rooms of Edinborough. In Ca-
nadian log cottages mothers sing their children to sleep
with them, and in the backwoods of America and the
sheep-walks of Australia the hardy emigrant hums them as
he works. In short, wherever a Scotch man goes, he carries

these songs in his memory with him, as a relic of the land
he has left behind him.

One of the best known of these poems is Auld Robin
Gray. It was written by Lady Anne Barnard.

When the sheep are in the fauld [1], when the kye's [2]
come hame,
And a' [3] the weary warld [4] to rest are gane [5],
The waes [6] o' my heart fa' [7] in showers frae [8] my e'e [9],
Unkent [10] by my gudeman [11] wha [12] sleeps sound by me.

Young Jamie lo'ed [13] me weel, and sought me for his
bride,
But saving [14] ae [15] crown piece he had naething [16] beside;
To make the crown a pound my Jamie gaed [17] to sea,
And the crown and the pound-they were baith [18] for me.

He hadna [19] been gane a twelvemounth and a day,
When my father brake his arm and the cow was stown [20]
away;
My mither [21] she fell sick — my Jamie was at sea,
And Auld Robin Gray came a courting, me.

My father could'na [22] wark [23], my mither couldna spin —
I toiled day and night, but their bread I couldna win;
And Rob maintained them baith, and, wi [24] tears in his e'e,
Said: „Jeanie, for their sakes, will ye no marry me?"

My heart it said na [25], for I looked for Jamie back,
But hard blew the winds, and his ship was a wrack,
His ship was a wrack — why didna Jamie die,
Or why am I spared to cry wae is me?

---

1 fold.   2 cattle.   3 all.   4 world.   5 gone.   6 woes.   7 fall.
8 from.   9 eye.   10 unknown.   11 husband.   12 who.   13 loved.
14 except.   15 one.   16 nothing.   17 went.   17 both.   19 had not.
20 stolen.   21 mother.   22 could not.   23 work.   24 with.   25 no.

My father urged me sair[26] — my mither didna speak,
But she looked in my face till my heart was like to break;
They gied[27] him my hand — my heart was in the sea —
And so Robin Gray he was gudeman to me.

I hadna' been his wife a week but only four,
When mournfu' as I sat on a stane[28] at my door,
I saw my Jamie's ghaist[29], I couldna think it he,
Till he said: „I' m come hame[30], love, to marry thee!"

O, sair sair did we greet[31], and mickle[32] say of a'
I gied him ae kiss, and bade him gang[33] awa' —
I wish I were dead, but I am na like to die,
For, though my heart is broken, I' m but young, wae
is me!

I gang like a ghaist, I carena much to spin,
I darena think o' Jamie for that wad[34] be a sin,
But I'll do my best a gude wife to be,
For Auld Robin Gray he's a kind gudeman to me.

Such were the poets who immediately preceeded Burns,
and such the songs which were sung over his cradle. We
must now enter into an examination of his works. *Robert
Burns* was born on the 25th Jan. 1759. His father seems
to have been a clever, sensible, and he certainly was an
honest and pious man. But his life had not been an easy
one, nor had it been fortunate. He had before the poets
birth been obliged to accept a place as gardener in the
service of the Laird of Fairly. Afterwards he took a small
farm which he cultivated with his own hands. When
Robert was six years old he was sent to school where he
learnt reading, writing and grammar. John Murdoch, the
teacher of this school, seems to have taken an interest in

26 much. 27 gave. 28 stone. 29 ghost. 30 home. 31 weep.
32 little. 33 go. 34 would.

him; for, when he took lessons in French, he used to teach his little pupil of a morning, what he himself had learnt the evening before. These lessons only lasted for a fortnight, as Robert had to return home. He took with him a French grammar, dictionary and a Télémaque, from which he taught himself French enough to be able to read any prose writer in that language. In after years he was very proud of this accomplishment, and often inserted French words and sentences in his letters. After Robert's return home, his father took his education into his own hands. He used to borrow books on all kinds of scientific subjects, and study them after the days work was over, in order that he might teach their contents to his children. In the mean time his son devoured every book that came within his reach. But this happy life was not to continue long. The farm did not pay, and a series of misfortunes overtook the poor family. The father's health too broke down, and Robert, at the age of fifteen, was the manager and chief labourer on the farm. At this time they were plunged in the deepest poverty, and it is probable that the hard labour, bad nourishment, and anxiety of this period was the cause of the descase which was never thoroughly cured. Robert however struggled bravely on. Strangely enough this was the time that he wrote his first poem. Here is his own account of the matter. „This kind of life — the cheerless gloom of a hermit, with the unceasing moil of a galley-slave, brought me to my sixteenth year; a little before which period I first committed the sin of Rhyme. You know our country custom of coupling a man and woman together as partners in the labours of the harvest. In my fifteenth autumn my partner was a bewitching creature a year younger than myself. My scarcity of English denies me the power of doing her justice in that language. .... How she caught the contagion, I cannot tell — but I never expressly said I loved

her. Indeed I did not know myself why I liked so much
to loiter behind with her, when returning in the evening
from our labours; why the tones of her voice made my heart-
strings thrill like an Aeolean harp; and particularly why my
pulse beat such a furious ratan when I looked and fingered
over her little hand to pick out the cruel nettle stings and
thistles. Among her other love-inspiring qualities, she sung
sweetly, and it was her favourite reel to which I attempted
giving an embodied vehicle in rhyme. I was not so pre-
sumptuous as to imagine that I could make verses like printed
ones, composed by men who had Greek and Latin; but my
girl sung a song, which was said to be composed by a small
country laird's son on one of his fathers maids, with whom
he was in love; and I saw no reason why I might not rhyme
as well as he, for, excepting that he could smear sheep,
and cast peats, his father living in the moorlands, he had
no more scholarcraft than myself."

At last the lease of the farm was out, and a new one
was taken. Here for four years things seemed to be getting
on better; but the old difficulties returned, and the poets
father was only saved from a debtors prison by death. The
whole care of the family now fell on the shoulders of Robert and his brother, and he bravely endeavoured to do his
duty; but misfortune after misfortune overtook him, until,
at last, he resolved to emigrate to Jamaica. Up to this
time Burns had never had more than £ 7. a year to live
upon, and he had never exceeded his income. This is a
sufficient proof that his life cannot, at that period, have
been very wild. His greatest excesses cannot have been
more than a dance now and then, and an occasional glass.
These however were, when united to habitual absence from
church, high crimes and misdemeanors in the eyes of the
rigid calvanists among whom he dwelt, and the clergy resolved to reprimand, and disgrace him publicly. Burns

ridiculed them in a series of satires which will never loose their sting, till religious hypocrisy, and intolerance have gone out of fashion. The poet at this period was attached, and even engaged to a girl in the neighbourhood, Jean A mour. Her father however would hear nothing of the engagement, and the connection had to be broken off.

Before leaving Europe Burns resolved to publish his poems. This he did by subscription. They were received with rapture by the public, and instead of starting for Jamaica, he was, in a few months, the darling of Edinburgh. The most flattering attentions were lavished upon him. He was carressed by the nobility, flattered by the wits, and courted by the ladies of that then brilliant capital. Spite of all however, he returned home, and married his old love. He sent nearly half of the money he received from his publisher to his mother, with the rest he took a farm. The brilliant society of Edinburgh forgot Burns, and hurried on to admire the next novelty, but it was not so easy for him to forget the witty and polished society he had for awhile enjoyed. After a time he began to neglect his farm, and every thing seemed to go wrong with him. Every tourist who passed his house endeavoured to catch a glimpse of the peasant poet. His neighbours, too, sought his company, and were enchanted by his wit and humour. Far too much has, I believe, been said of the poets dissipation. There can be no doubt that he, like most people of that age, sometimes drank a glass too much, but the straitlaced Calvinists among whom he lived were only too glad „to find or forge a fault" in the satirist who had so mercilessly chastised their intolerance and hypocrisy. It is certain however that he soon became disgusted with farming, and that it was a great relief to him when a friend procured him a place in the Excise. His salary was never more than L. 70 a year, but on this he resolved to life, and to hope for promotion. At this time the French revolution was

filling Europe with hope and terror. Burns was passionately
attached to the cause of the French people, and eagerly
defended them. Information as to his sentiments was given
to the Board of Excise, and he received a severe reprimand.
This was a hard blow to a mind so proud and sensitive as
his. A report was spread that he had lost his situation,
and a friend proposed a subscription in his favour, but
Burns refused the offer in a very characteristic letter:

„The partiality of my countrymen has brought me forward as a man of genius, and given me a character to
support. In the Poet I have avowed manly and independent
sentiments, which I hope have been found in the man. Reasons of no less weight than the support of a wife and
children, have pointed out my present occupation as the
only eligible line of life within my reach. Still my honest
fame is my dearest concern, and a thousand times have I
trembled at the idea of the degrading epithets that malice or
miss representation may affix to my name. Often, in blasting
anticipation, have I listened to some future hackney scribb-
ler, with the heavy malice of savage stupidity, exultingly
asserting that Burns, notwithstanding the fanfaronade of
independence to be found in his works, and after having
been held up in public view and to public estimation as
a man of some genius, yet, quite destitute of resources
within himself to support his borrowed dignity, dwindled
into a paltry exciseman and slunk out the rest of his insignificant existence in the meanest of pursuits and among
the lowest of mankind.

„In your illustrious hands, Sir, permit me to lodge my
strong disavowal and defiance of such slanderous falsehoods.
Burns was a poor man from his birth, and an exciseman by
necessity; but — I will say it! — The sterling of his honest
worth poverty could not debase, and his independent British
spirit oppression might bend, but could not subdue.“

One of the last acts of his life was tore-copy this letter,

and to place it carefully among his MSS., that it might serve as an eternal protest against slander.

All hope of promotion was now at an end, and the story of the rest of his life is easily told. He was taken severily ill soon after, and never quite recovered. On his death-bed he was tormented by anxiety for his wife and children; but he was soothed by the care, love, and forgiveness of his wife, whose constant patience, forbearance, and tenderness did all that could be done to comfort him. He died on the 22nd of July 1796.

We must now proceed to an examination of his works. Foremost among them stands Tam o' Shanter, a tale written in broad Scotch. It is a masterpiece in its way, the best story of the kind in our literature, with the exception of those of Chaucer. The poem commences with a description of an Inn at Ayr. It is a market-night and Tam is seated at the fire side by Johnny:

> His ancient trusty drouthy crony
> Tam lo'ed him like a vera brither,
> They had been fou for weeks thegither.
> The night drave on wi' sangs and clatter
> And ay the ale was growing better;
> The souter tauld his queerest stories;
> The landlords laugh was ready chorus.
> The storm without might rair and ristle,
> Tam did na mind the storm a whistle.
> His wife mean while was sitting at home
> Gath'ring her brows like gath'ring storm,
> Nursing her wrath to keep it warm.

So the evening passes away and Tam finds at last that it is time to go home. It's a wild stormy night, a perfect huricane, thunder, lightning and rain:

> That night a child might understand,
> The Deil had business on his hand.

The way too is dismal enough, every turning has been the

scene of some unnatural crime, or fearful accident. But
Tam has a good mare under him, and is well wrapt up and
as to spirits he has drank too much good ale and whisky to
care for them. So, humming one old song after another,
and turning round every now and then prudently lest the
ghosts should catch him unawares, he rides safely on, till
he comes within sight of Alloway Church, a celebrated gathering place of the witches. When lo! the whole church
is in a blaze. This frightens Tam's horse, who stands still,
but her owner, with all the bravery of a glass or two
too much, urges her on and peeps in. There a strange
sight presents itself to him. The devil himself is enthroned
in the midst of the church, playing the bag-pipes with all
his might, while round him all the witches of the whole
country side hurry, and leap, and spring, in a fiendish
dance. The dead stand around in their open coffins, each
holding a light in the right hand. The other particulars of
the ghastly scene I need not discribe. For a time Tam looks
on in silence, while Old Nick plays ever louder and quicker,
and the dance becomes ever wilder and madder. But as ill
luck would have it, among the hideous crew there was
one pretty face, and that turned his head. It was Nannie,
who had joined the company for the first time that night,
and who outdid all the rest of the dancers. At last, when
the riot is at the height, Tam hollows out his applause. In
a moment all the lights are extinguished, and the fiendish
crew rush out upon Tam, with Nannie at their head. Away
rushes the horse with Tam on her back, and the witches at
her heels. If she can get across the bridge, they are safe,
for witches and fiends cant pass running water. Just as she
reaches it, however, Nannie, who is far in advance of the
rest, catches her by the tail —

> But little wist she Maggie's mettle —
> Ae spring brought aff her master hail,
> And left behind her ain grey tail.

Such is a slight sketch of the story of Tam o' Shanter. The whole piece is written with inimitable spirit and humour. It is treated so realistically, that even the wild and unearthly dance seems a simple matter of history. There are too strange touches of pathos in the wild tale. Such are the few lines the author addresses to Nannie.

> A little kenn'd[1] thy reverend grannie,
> The sark[2] she coft[3] for her wee[4] Nannie,
> Wi twa[5] pund[6] Scots (twas a' her riches)
> Wad ever grace a dance of witches.

In short, in variety, life, and artistic execution it takes a high place among Burns's poems.

The Cotter's Saturday night is a strange contrast to Tam o' Shanter. It is the expression of the strict Calvinism which has become a national characteristic of Scotland. Burns has painted it, in this poem, with a very loving hand. Saturday evening is an important time to the peasantry of Scotland. The implements of work have been laid aside, early in the afternoon, and the evening is spent in preparation for the Sunday. The various members of the family, if possible, meet together, and the earnestness of the „Sabbath", without its painful strictness, seems to sanctify the last hours of the week. It is clear that such a subject is not unpoetical, but it owes a great part of its charm to early associations. Perhaps no one but a Scotchman can thoroughly enjoy this poem. I must confess, I am at a loss to understand the rapture with which it is often spoken of. Yet it is a poem of great beauty, one of the best idylls in our language, but then our literature is not rich in idylls. Putting the subject aside, and examining the execution alone, we shall find I think, that it has two great faults. An idyll is, by its nature, as objective as an epic. Every intrusion of the authors person or opinion breaks the charm,

---

1 knew. 2 shirt. 3 bought. 4 little. 5 two. 6 pounds.

because it is out of tone with the rest of the picture. So
we find in the most beautiful of modern idylls, „Hermann
and Dorothea“, and „Alexis and Dora“, that the poet keeps
himself quite out of sight. No one could have done this
better than Burns had he been so inclined. He has done it in
„the Jolly beggars“, in „Hallowe'en“, and in many other
poems. But in the „Cotters Saturday night“ he takes the tone
of Cowper, he preaches and reflects. He tells us so often how
much he admires the Cotter and his family, that we ca'nt
help having an unpleasant feeling that perhaps they are
doing it all to be admired. The simple rustic grace of the
idyll is wanting. In fact, the subject was not exactly suited
to the character of Burns; he had too much of the gay,
sensuous nature of the artist about him to be a real Cal-
vinist, or to sympathise deeply with the exaggerated ideality, and hard ascetism of that sect. But he was a peasant,
and he admired the honest, hard working, pious ways of his
neighbours. He had gone to the dancing-school against his
father's will, he had ` lived for years in constant contention
with him because of his love for gaiety; yet he seems to
have looked on him as one of the best and noblest of mankind. His quick eye saw the various poetic beauties of the
Saturday evening, and he endeavoured to weave them into
a poem; but it was an endeavor, and not the natural out-
pouring of his heart. He seems to me, too, to have been
unfortunate in his choice of rhythm. The „Cotters Saturday
night“ is written in the Spensorean stanza. This is a highly
complex and melodious form of verse excellently suited for
the aërial dreams of the fairy Queen, but much too artificial
for such a subject as this. In short, this poem, though it
has many beauties, does not seem to me nearly equal to the
best of his works. „Hallowe'en“ shows what Burns could do
in this line when the subject suited him. It takes its name
from a Scotch festival, and the different customs are sketched
with great truth and humour. The satirical poems of Burns

were mostly personal, or directed against the church authorities. They are terribly biting and cruel, and are pervaded
by a rich vein of humor. To understand the bitterness of
hatred which they breathe, we must remember that the
church of Scotland was at that period, and alas in many
places still is, the most bigotted of sects. Buckle, who of
all English historians has the greatest grasp of mind and
width of reading, gives it as his deliberate opinion, that no
land in Europe, with the sole exception of Spain, is so so-
rely priestridden as Scotland. The authorities of the Kirk
endeavoured to crush Burns, so that he is scarcely to be
blamed for holding up their names to eternal ignominy. Closely connected with but infinitely superior to these poems is
the „Address to the Deil", a tragicomical poem of great beauty
and power. Burns's epigrams are, for the most part, weak
and pointless. „The jolly beggars" is an excellent picture of
low life. It is a series of songs connected by short pieces
of narrative. The characters of the singers are finely distinguished by a few broad lines and simple touches, and the
songs are fine specimens of roaring merriment.

But it is as a lyric poet that Burns is greatest. As a
narrative, descriptive, and satirical poet he had predecessors,
and has had successors, who may dispute his right to the
highest place. As a song writer he stands alone. Chaucer is
not more surely the greatest of our tale-tellers, nor Shakespeare more certainly the first of our dramatists, than
Burns is the greatest of our lyrical poets. In his songs
there is no struggle after effect, no rhetoric, no selfcon-
sciousness. They are simply songs, the expression of strong
natural feeling, and no more. This is what has made them
so widely popular. They are sung in every Scotch cottage,
they are to be found beside the Bible on every peasant's
bookshelf, and were every copy of his works to be destroyed, all his songs might, I believe, in twenty years
time be collected by word of mouth from the Scotch pea-

santry. This cannot be said of any other English writer
and it is the highest praise that can be given to a lyric
poet. His songs sprung from the heart of the people, and
have entered so deeply into the national life, that it is almost as easy to imagine an England without Shakespeare,
as a Scotland without Burns.

B O O K II.

1800 — 1830.

———

CHAPTER I.

We must now enter into an examination of our literature during the second period which falls under our consideration. This age may be said to begin with the century, and
to end with the death of Scott, in 1832. It differs in many
important respects from that which preceeded it. The latter
was, as we have seen, an age of struggle. The cold regularity
of the classical school had been attacked and conquered by
a few men of genius. This struggle had not, as in Germany,
been fought by the critics, but by the poets. They had destroyed the old taste by creating a new one; and it was not till
this taste had been embodied in works of art that the critics
declared in its favour. In Germany a single man, Lessing,
attacked and destroyed an absurd code of literary laws, and
set poetry free from the chains that had bound her. In England the same work was done by *Chatterton*, *Percy*, and
Cowper. But the way in which it was done was very different. Lessing measured the authors of the classical school by
the literature that they themselves had chosen, and found
them wanting. Percy appealed to another standard, and repub-
lished our ancient poems. He turned from Greece to the England of the Elizabethan and pre-Elizabethan age. Hence
the different directions which the two literatures took as soon
as they were freed from their trammels. That of Germany
passed through the lofty and somewhat highflown verses of
Klopstock and the would-be classicism of Wieland, to the
Grecian purity of Goethe. The first original productions

of our poetry, on the other hand, were tales moulded on the old metrical romances. We had alas no Goethe to direct and enoble our poetry, to modify and moderate its excentricities, to unite its beauties and to make it of European interest. And here we cannot help asking how it was that the poets of this period chose the metrical romances rather than the Elizabethan drama as their models. This question has, I believe, never been satisfactorily answered. All I can do is to throw out a few hints ou the subject. At first sight their choice between the two literatures seems a strange one. Our metrical romances, as a whole, are certainly not superior to those of France and Germany, while our drama stands alone. Perhaps this was one of the very reasons that prevented it being more widely imitated. The poets of the first half of the present century could not hope to write plays that could surpass, or even equal those of Shakespeare and his contemporaries; whereas they might well hope to write poems in a new or at least forgotten style that would deserve and receive applause. But the real reason of their choice lay. I believe, principally in the nature of their own talents and character, and in the age in which they lived. The first of these we shall examine when we come to speak of the great poets separately, the second we must now glance at for a few minutes. In the Elizabethan age books had been scarce and dear and but a small proportion of the inhabitants of England could read and write. Yet the craving after intellectual food was deeper and more widely extended then, than at almost any other period of our history. This was a necessary result of the sudden changes which had been wrought by the Reformation. In England these changes had not, as in Germany and Scotland, originated in the people. It was the government of the country which had ordered that all should be changed, and the people had looked on with a-mazement while their churches were plundered, and the most beautiful of pictures, and the holiest of relics were commit-

ted to the flames. The Queen of Heaven had been cast down
from her high place. The priests whom they had loved and
reverenced, who had been their counsellors in difficulty and
their comforters in woe, were banished as traitors from the
shores of England. The monasteries, which had been the
granaries of the poor, had passed from the holy orders to
which they had belonged. The people had seen Sir Thomas
More led out to execution for holding doctrines which, but
a short time before, none of them had doubted to be the
truth of God. Again, they had seen the fires of Smithfield
lighted, and the leaders of the reformation dying there. They
had seen the purest and the holiest of both parties seal their
testimony with their blood, and had heard them appeal from
their mortal judges to the same God and the same Christ.
Such scenes could not but make the most careless thoughtful.
It was this that caused the hunger after intellectual food of
which I have spoken. But, as I have already said, books
were rare and dear. In the churches theological questions
were treated, and the churches were crowded; but the interest of the people was not confined to Theology. Hence the
influence of the theatres at that period, and the throngs
with which they were crowded. The age of Byron and Scott
was not entirely dissimilar to that of Shakspeare. Once
more the old and the new had met in a death-struggle. The
French monarchy had been overthrown, and it had dragged
down the church and aristocracy with it in its fall. A new
gospel had been proclaimed at Paris which had made a thousand eyes beam brighter and a thousand hearts beat more
quickly. Prisoners had smiled in their dungeons, while
monarchs trembled on their thrones. A new truth had been
proclaimed, a new age was born. Hence we find that this
period was one of unusual intellectual activity in the whole
of the civilized world. But, in many respects, the age of
the reformation and that of the revolution were vastly different. Only a few of these points of difference concern us

now. The commencement of the nineteenth century had
newspapers, magazines, reviews, and novels, the seventeenth century had none of these things. Hence the interest, which had formerly centred on the drama, was divided into a thousand chanels, and the theatre, of all intellectual amusements, profited least by the newly awakened
interest. A few facts prove beyond a doubt that this was
the case. The dramatist was the only author, in the age of
Elizabeth, who could hope to live by the sale of his writings.
Any other poet had to seek out some rich nobleman or cour-
tier, who was willing to support a man of genius for the sake
of his genius alone, or to pay a high price for a few pages of
graceful flattery. In the age of Scott play-writers were the
worst paid of literary drudges. The theatre, too, was no
longer looked upon with anything like the respect it had
once enjoyed. It was no longer respected as a teacher and
guide. It was considered at best but an innocent, and many
thought it a sinful amusement. Nor can this be wondered
at. The frivolity and ribaldry of the comic dramatists of
the Restoration had desecrated the boards that the genius
of Shakspeare and Fletcher had once hallowed. But, though
this dislike to the theatre was excusable, it was not the less
injurious. Being looked upon as a mere luxury the theatres
became luxurious. Two great buildings took the place of the
19 playhouses, which had flourished in London in the age
of Elizabeth. There can be no doubt that these theatres
where much more commodious, and that their decorations
were much more splendid, than those of the old playhouses
had been. But to pay for this, the prices of admission were
necessarily high. Thus it became impossible for the lower
and middle classes to frequent them as they had once done.
A visit to the play was considered a treat for special occa-
sions, an expense which could only be incurred once or
twice in the year. Thus the taste of the public was not educated as it had formerly been, This was an incalculable

loss, and it was attended by another of almost equal extent. A play which took had often a run of fifty or a hundred nights, which would have been impossible if the same people had frequently visited the theatre. Thus there was but a small demand for new plays, and this demand has been principally supplied by bad adaptations of old English plays and French farces. This circumstance has, I believe, done much to discourage our modern authors, and has prevented many of them trying their powers as dramatists.

Another evil has still to be mentioned. Almost all great dramatists have been nearly connected with the stage. Those of the Elizabethan age were, almost without an exception, either actors themselves, or the constant companions of actors. The necessity of such an acquaintance with the stage is evident from the number of great poets who, from want of it, have been unable to master the technicalities of the theatre. But in modern times it is almost impossible for an English author of eminence to form such a connection. The position of authors in society has risen since the days of Elizabeth. This is partly owing, no doubt, to the much larger sums that are paid for literary work; but it is, in an equal degree, to be attributed to the much higher request in which literature stands among men of all classes. But the position of our actors has altered for the worse, rather than the better. They are excluded from society. The fact of a person being on the stage is looked upon, by a great part of our middle classes, as a disgrace, which can hardly be atoned for by the union of the most brilliant genius, and the most unsullied character. Hence men of taste and education shrink from the profession of an actor, unless they are spurred on to it by the high instinct of genius. This has done much to prevent our poets forming close connexions with the stage.

These are I think the principle reasons why no dramatist of high standing is to be found among our modern poets. Since we have already entered, at such a length, into an exa-

mination of our modern stage, we may as well finish what
we have to say about it before going further. The English
stage has, I believe, sunk to a lower level than that of either
Germany or France. Not that our greatest living actors may
not take a place beside those of other countries, but because
the average play of our second or third rate actors is much
worse. In fact our stage suffers from two great evils. The
management of a theatre is either looked upon as a purely
mercantile speculation, or it falls into the hands of a single
actor. The evils in both cases are great and nearly the same.
The manager, in the first case, generally knows but little
of dramatic art, and in order to attract a large audience,
he engages one or two of the most popular actors he can
find. Their names are printed in large type on the play-
bills, plays are written and arranged to suit them, and
the whole world goes not to see Othello, but to see M^r such
a one as Jago, or Miss so and so as Desdemona. If the
manager be an actor we are not much better off. He is generally a man of known and acknowledged talent, and he
supposes, rightly enough, that when we come to his theatre
we wish to see him. He consequently engages one or two
actors and actresses of some celebrity, and gives the minor
parts to people who have about as much claim to the name
of actors as a signboard painter has to that of an artist. It
follows, as a matter of course, that the less that is seen
of them the better, and the drama is cut down into little
more than a series of dialogues and monologues. Now every
great dramatist, when he writes a play, writes it as a whole.
Each character has its proper part, and all the parts are
well proportioned, and carefully put together. Nothing can
be left out, and nothing added without marring the effect.
This is the case with Shakespeare more than perhaps with
any other modern writer, except Goethe. Some of his dramas cannot, for various reasons, be produced on the stage
as they were in his time, but no alteration should be under-

taken without the greatest care and forethought. His plays
should not be treated as waste paper on which every bungler
may try his scissors. But we are perhaps still worse off when
the whole of the drama is given, for the minor characters
serve no purpose, in many London theatres, but that of
destroying the effect intended by the poet. It is this that
frightens many people of taste from our theatres, and makes
others prefer seeing farces and sensational pieces to the
great masterworks with which our literature is supplied.
To people of a sensitively refined taste it seems almost a des-
ecration to see Lear and Hamlet as they are too often given
on the English stage. This is, I think, the reason why the
great dramas of the Elizabethan age are banished from our
theatres, to make room for third-rate French comedies, and
bad dramatizations of sensational novels. Endeavours have
been made to stop the downward course of our theatres. Mac-
ready battled earnestly with the depraved taste of his day
and he did something to raise the tone of the theatre, but his
work died away almost as soon as he left the stage. Then
came Charles Kean who applied his great genius and refined
taste to the great end of reestablishing Shakspeare on the
stage. While he was manager of the Princess's we could boast,
that there was at least one theatre in London in which the
works of the greatest of our dramatists were produced un-
mangled, and so as not to offend the most fastidious taste.
But with his retirement the effects of his long work passed
away, and our theatres seem now to have sunk to as low a
level as ever. Nor can we hope for a lasting improvement until the taste of the public has improved. I have already said
that in England the drama has almost ceased to be considered
an art, and that it is looked upon as at best a harmless way
of killing time; yet no art has a larger scope or a higher
mission. It unites music, poetry, and painting. It gives life
to pictures, and form to words. A great part of the religious
public of England turns from it with disgust, and yet, pro-

perly employed, it would be the mightiest instrument of ef-
fecting the highest of their ends, the education of the people.
We hear constant complaints that, while the lower classes
are being enticed and allured into schools and evening classes, while they are being crammed with chemistry, and mathematics, and immense sums are being spent on mechanics
institutes and libraries, their manners and morals remain
almost unaltered.   As if a perfect acquaintance with the
elements must necessarily make a man a good father, or a
knowledge of equations prevent him beating his wife! It is
a fact that all philantropists would do well to remember that
mere knowledge does nothing towards refining the mind. That
is the province of Art; and lyrical and dramatic poetry are
the only branches of art which, in our age, can make any
deep impression on the mind of the people.   I am convinced
that a series of good dramas, well acted, would do more to
educate the people than a dozen courses of lectures, beneficial as
they doubtlessly are.   When the English public learns these
facts, when it ceases to look upon the drama as a frivolous
amusement, and begins to reverence it as a high and holy
art, when our religious public has discovered that the theatre
is not the „devils chapel“ but the temple of that which is
best and noblest in man; when our actors begin to reverence
their calling, and discover how high their mission is, then —
and not till then — can we hope to have in England such man-
agers as Dingelstedt, and actors that are worthy of such a
manager.

The literature of England, during the first thirty years
of the present century, was uncommonly brilliant. No period
in our history, with the one exception of the age of Elizabeth, has an equal number of poets to boast of. None of
them, it is true, were of the very first rank, but many
stood high in the second. Byron and Scott have European
reputations, and Wordsworth, Shelley, and Keats were scarcely inferior to them in poetical genius. In examining the

works of these writers it will, I think, be better to devide them into groups than to follow the strictly chronological order.

We may devide them into three great groups, each of which will be found to correspond with one of the leaders of our literary reformation. The first consists of those poets who chose heroic subjects, and who may be looked upon as the followers of Percy. They turned away from common everyday-life, and delighted in portraying distant lands and ages. The second on the other hand confined themselves, for the most part, to modern subjects. They were the intellectual successors of Cowper. This school may be said to have split into two. The one party, under the leadership of Crabbe, (b. 1754. d. 1832) followed a realistic method. They have had so slight an influence on our literature that they will not claim any farther notice. Their great fault was that they merely reproduced nature, without idealizing it. The second party, that of Wordsworth, after passing through various phases, became, like Cowper, reflective or, as they called themselves, philosophic poets. The third group, of whom Chatterton may be considered the forerunner, indulged in splendid and gorgeous dreams. They built, so to speak, cloud-palaces, which were grand, beautiful, and unreal. The first of these three groups was the most brilliant, and gained the greatest, and most immediate popularity; the last two have exerted by far the most permanent influence over our poetry.

This classification is of course arbitrary, but it may serve our purpose which is to get a clear view of the greatest poets of the age. Each of the schools produced men who were far greater than the poet of the last century whose name we have connected with them; no one for instance would think of comparing Cowper with Wordsworth. There are several poets with whom it is difficult to deal; the principal of these is Coleridge who belonged to all three schools.

4 *

We shall leave him in the place that is most frequently given
him — by Wordsworth.

CHAPTER II.

The first of the groups, into which we have divided
the poets of our second period contains *Scott, Byron* and
Moore. These poets, though the difference between them is
wide, were more nearly related to each other than to any of
their contemporaries. We must now proceed to examine their
works severally.

Sir *Walter Scott* was born in Edinburgh, the 15th of
August 1771. He was sent, on account of ill health, while
very young, to live with his grand-father in the country.
Here the wild mountain-scenery, and the Border-tales and
ballads made a deep impression upon him. At the age of
thirteen he first read Percy's „Reliques“, a book which always remained a great favourite of his. Scotts father was
a presbyterian, and the first of his verses which have been
preserved are of a religious cast. He was educated at the
High school and University of Edinburgh, after which he
studied for the bar, and was called in his twenty-first year.
His studies however did not prevent him making frequent
journeys into the country during which he observed the manners, and collected the legends and songs of the peasantry.
At this time the intellectual society of Edinburgh had begun to take a deep interest in the literature of Germany.
Scott became more deeply interested in it than almost any
one else. He translated „Leonore“ and the „Wild Huntsman“
in 1796. On the 24th of December of the following year he
married Charlotte Margaret Carpenter a young lady of French
extraction. He still continued his German studies and in
1799 he published a translation of „Goetz von Berlichingen.“

His next work was the „Minstrelsy of the Scottish Border", a collection of old songs and ballads, which he had gathered in his frequent excursions. He soon after edited and publish ed an old metrical romance, „Sir Tristrem". Thus we see that three distinct influences had been, up to this time, acting on Scott's mind; they were firstly the ballad-literature of the Border, with its heroism, tenderness and truth, secondly the German literature, which was then in the flush of youthful power, and lastly the old metrical romances, with their wildly imaginative fancy and grace. Under the influence of these three his mind mas formed, and their influence over the whole of our modern literature can hardly be estimated too highly.

Scotts next work was an original poem, „The Lay of the Last Minstrel", This poem at once raised him to a high place among living poets. It is a border-story of the sixteenth century. The tale partakes of the character both of the metrical romance and the ballad. It is more ornate than the last, more simple.forcible and natural than the first usually were. Everywhere we find the skill in description, and the music of rhythm, which were so peculiar to Scott. These beauties ensured the poem an imense success. His next work, „Marmion" appeared in 1808. It wants the unity of the „Lay", but it has passages of far higher beauty than the earlier poem contains. The great fault of the poem was pointed out by Jeffreys at its first appearance. It lies in the character of the hero. Not that Marmion is falsely drawn. Such characters may, and probably have existed. It lies in its opposition to the character and tone of the poem. The tale, like all Scott's stories, is full of the wild heroism and chivalrous sense of honor which distinguishes the literature of the middle ages. The hero of such a tale might have committed any violent crime, he might have been cruel, sensual, and revengeful, but he should not have been mean and deceitful. The romance-writers of the middle ages taught

that courage and honesty, and fraud and cowardice went
together; and, though they were doubtless psychologically
wrong, they were aesthetically right in doing so. But Marmion is a hero and a villain, a knight and a forger. Byron
translated this criticism into a series of biting epigrams.

„Next view in state, proud prancing on his roan,
The golden - crested haughty Marmion,
Now forging scrolls, now foremost in the fight,
Not quite a felon, yet but half a knight,
The gibbet or the field prepared to grace,
A mighty mixture of the great and base.

Yet Marmion was a poem of great originality and
power. The description of the battlefield and the death of
Marmion is one of the finest poetical passages of the kind in
our language. It was followed (1810) by the „Lady of the
Lake“, which was still more popular than its predecessors.
The descriptions of scenery in this poem are more brilliant
and executed with greater skill than in either of the other
poems, and the story is interesting and well told; but the
characters want the distinctness and force of the earlier poems
with the one exception of Roderik Dhu, the Highland chief,
whose bravery honour and generosity are well drawn, and
powerfully contrasted with his inplacable hatred. He is one
of those characters which Byron delighted to draw dark,
gloomy and sublime as the mountains among which he moves.
The poems which followed are written in the same style, but
they are not to be compared with the first three. The Lord
of the Isles is the best of them. It is an attempt to tell the
story of Bruce but, with the exception of one or two brilliant
passages, the poem is scarcely worthy of its author.

As soon as Scott found that his poems began to pall on
the public taste, and that his genius in verse was beginning
to wane, he resolved to abandon poetry forever. But he
had no intention of leaving off writing. In 1814 he publish-

ed his first prose romance, „Waverly". This novel is a tale
of Scotch life during the insurrection of 1745. The subject,
style and characters were entirely new. No more striking
scene or time could have been chosen. The rugged mountains
of the Scotch highlands, the half patriarchal, half feudal manners of their inhabitants, and the wild pomp and chivalrous
devotion of the clans were new to English readers. The time
too was one of the most strikingly romantic in the history of
Scotland. It was the last gathering of the clans, the last
hopeless but chivalrous struggle of the house of Stuart to
regain its birthright. The period was one of glaring contrasts. It was as if the middle ages, with their enthusiasm,
loyalty, and well marked individuality, had declared war
with the civilization, the science, and organization of modern times. There could be no doubt that the new must be
victorious over the old, and it was well that it should be so,
but few can help sympathizing with the heroism and self devotion of the weaker party. The time too was sufficiently distant
to have cooled down all party hatred and yet near enough to
have something of modern interest. Many were still alive
who could remember the hope or fear with which they heard
that the highlanders were on the march, and that the ban-
ner of the Stuarts was once again unfurled. But they were
old men now, new interests had banished the old question
from their minds, and they looked back at it as one of the
dreams of their youth. The whole style of the novel was very
different to any that had gone before it. We had had great
novelists before. The names of Fielding, Sterne and Smollet
will be remembered, and their works will be read as long
as the English language endures. But their tales are for the
most part humourous and they are confined to private life. No
great historical event had before the time of Scott been treated by a novelist of genius. In Waverley all the heroism
and enthusiasm, all the high interests and passions which had
before been confined to the tragedy were brought into play,

and toned down and contrasted with passages of refined and delicate humor. Besides the spirit of Waverley was very different to that of our earlier novelists. It breathed the chivalrous feelings of its heroes. Their loyalty, generosity, and love of danger for its own sake seemed to be as much parts of the authors character as of their own. His interest in them seemed to be the sympathy of a kindred nature. All these things contributed to make the book universally popular. Old men still remember how eagerly it was bought and read by people of all classes. Scott had not affixed his name to it from fear that his poetical fame might be endangered by an attempt in an entirely new branch of literature, and he kept up his incognito. A long series of prose romances followed Waverly and occupied his time from 1814 to 1831. Scott had in his own character something of the romance he delighted in depicting. Born himself of an old, though not of a noble family, he longed to be the father of a race which might take its place among the old Border-families. With this view he had engaged in a printing and publishing speculation which never brought him much money. Now, with the proceeds of his novels, he bought a princely estate. He spent about £ 35,000 in the purchase of land, and more than £ 5000 in improving it. He then built his celebrated mansion Abbotsford which certainly did not cost less than £ 20,000. Here he lived in a princely style „doing the honours for all Scottland." His house was crowded with guests whom he entertained as if he had been the richest nobleman in the country. In 1820 George IV conferred on him the honour of the Baronetcy. At this time he used to rise early and devote his mornings to writing, the rest of the day he spent in riding round his estate and superintending improvements, or in the company of his guests. Yet he never exceeded his income, and this income was almost entirely the product of his literary labours. Every thing that he had desired now seemed to be within his reach, and he could look forward with all but certainty to the fulfilment of his hopes. In 1825 however the bankruptcy of Constable brought losses of £ 60,000 on the poet. On the following year the publishing speculation in which he had been engaged failed and he found himself in debt to the amount of £ 117,000. This was a heavy blow to Scott, but he bore it nobly, he refused to make any composition with his creditors and declared his intention of paying the whole sum, demanding only time to do it in. He sold his town house in Edinburgh and retired to Abbotsford, where he now lived very simply. In four years he had paid off the sum of £ 70,000.

The first great work which he thus wrote under the pressure of necessity was the Life of Napoleon. This book excited great expectation in the whole of Europe. The English government had, it was said, supplied the materials. Scott would now furnish a masterpiece, it was supposed, which would throw all his former works into the shade. The wisest, it is true, shook their heads. They remembered that Scott was an Englishman and a Tory, and they hinted that his prejudices were stronger than those of any great living author. Some indeed whispered that he had been bought by the government, others answered that there had been no need of buying. The public had not long to wait; in a year the work appeared. It is needless to say that it was a complete failure. No life of Napoleon could then have been written which would have satisfied all, or perhaps any party. The time was not then, perhaps it is not yet come, when this man could be fairly judged, and Scott was of all men the most unfitted for the task. By birth he was a Scotchman, by inclination an antiquarian, in feelings and politics a Tory. How could a man who had spent his life in casting the brightest hues of romance over the history of the past, whose great aim in life it had been to found a family which at some distant period might take its place among the aristocracy, and who was even now working like a slave to pay off with

mercantile exactness a debt which the strictest moralist
would never have blamed him for compounding, sympathise
with this wonder of the nineteenth century, this Titan child
of the revolution, who trampled with equal carelessness on
the crowns of kings and the rights of nations? He was unfitted, alike by his virtues and his weaknesses, for doing so.
Nor could he understand even the circumstances in which
Napoleon had been placed. The wild enthusiasm of the re-
volutionists was incomprehensible to him. He shrank from
it as from an infectious madness. He could not see that the
great leaders of the revolution were men who were intox-
icated with an idea, who were fighting desperately for a
hope which, if it was distant and unachievable, was at least
noble and pure. Scott approaches this giant representative
of the revolution, this incarnation of the French people with
a look of puzzled wonder, he measures him with his little
foot-rule and finds him wanting, he judges him by the laws
against which his whole life had been a protest and finds him
guilty. All this was natural — unavoidable, but Heine very
justly remarks that it was strange that so clever a portrait-
painter as Scott should not have been able to give a clear
idea even of the external appearance of Napoleon. Yet perhaps after all even that was natural, and, though we may
regret Scott's failure, we shall hardly blame him for it.

The life of Napoleon was followed by several new novels which, though greatly inferior to the earlier volumes
of the series, were received with great applause by the public. These works brought in money and Scott had reason to
hope that his debts would soon be paid, and that he should
be able to return again to the way of life which he had found
so congenial. But his constitution, though remarkably strong,
could not support the amount of mental exertion which he
had undergone. In 1830 he had an attack of paralysis and,
from that time, his health continued to decline. He would not
however give up his literary labours until he became too

weak to continue them. In 1831 he went to Italy, in the hope that a change of air and scene might benefit his health. It came too late. He returned to Abbotsford only to die. He breathed his last on the 21st of September 1832.

On considering Sir Walter Scott's works as a whole, the first thing that strikes us is their healthy moral tone. Their purity is no doubt partly owing to the age in which he lived. A hundred, nay fifty years before, a lady who could not read or write was no curiosity, good spelling was looked upon with suspicion, and a young lady who read much was sure to get the character of a pedant, and to be shunned as a blue-stocking. Swift, Fielding and Sterne wrote for men alone, so they wrote loosely. As soon as the education of ladies improved; and they began to read the novels of the day, the tone of works of imagination improved. All looseness of thougt or expression was banished from our lighter literature, so that Scott is deserving of no particular praise on that account. But seven other devils, worse than the former, seemed to have taken the place of the one that was cast out. I believe that there never was a period, except that which immediately succeeded the restoration, in which our literature was so beset with unhealthy influences as it was during the first part of the present century. Egotistical misanthropy and overstrained sentimentality walked hand in hand. On one side their was a deification of crime, on the other a sickly delicacy that would not believe that vice existed. Here Atheism strutted her little hour upon the stage, there a piety which was scarcely less blasphemous stood praying at the corners of the streets. Everywhere there was cant and hypocrisy. Of all these moral diseases Scott was singularly free. The moral tone of his writings is always manly and open. He calls right and wrong by their proper names. He paints men as they are, neither angels nor devils, and does not preach about them. He had none of the unhealthy love of paradox which marred the works of

Byron and many others among his contemporaries. These
are moral qualities which can scarcely be praised too highly.
He has had his reward. His books are in every library and
on every table, and they have done more to educate the
young people of England than all other works of fiction taken together.

When we look at them critically and from an aesthetical
point of view, we find that, spite of the great power and
the many beauties of his writings, we cannot give him a
place among the very greatest of our poets. No poet, not
even Shakespeare or Goethe, ever showed a greater power in
grouping his characters. They are arranged naturaly and yet
with the clearest possible perception of effect. They are contrasted with a masterly skill and placed amid scenes exactly
fitted to be the back-grounds of such groups. In what artists call the massing of colour he is unsurpassed. The tale
runs on through a ceaseless variety of incident. Scene succeeds scene in unending variety, yet there is no dissonance,
no glaring want of harmony. He is not, it is true, a polished
writer, nor are the various details studied and elaborated
with the untiring patience of Hawthorne. He loves broad
effects, he delights like Rubens in firm, forcible lines. In
the description of scenery, too, he has never been surpassed.
His pictures have almost geographical truth. Yet they have
none of the tedious minuteness which often wearies us in
other writers. He knows what to say and what to leave un-
said. Above all, his pictures both of men and things are
distinct. They stand out clearly from the canvas, their outlines are sharp, and their colouring well marked. This is one
of the things which separate him so widely from the writers
of the romantic school, who were his German contemporaries — from De la Motte Fouque'for example. If we compare
the „Zauberring“ with „Ivanhoe“, for example, we find that
the effect which the German romance produces is caused for
the most part by the sentiments and feelings which are the

ground-tone of the tale. The scenes and figures are bathed
in the rosy hues of sunset, and the dim twilight of evening.
It is this dim religious light, this indistinctness which gives
the story its indescribable charm. Its beauty, like that
of a fairy tale, of the Arabian nights for example, owes
much to its distance from us. Scotts novel, on the other
hand, and it is far from being his best, fascinates by the realism of his treatment. He conjures up the middle ages and
places them before us, and we are surprised and pleased to
find that they were so like our own. The object of Scott too
was quite different from that of the German romantic school.
He tried to reproduce the past as it had really been, and
drew his materials from old chronicles, antiquities, and ballads. They endeavoured to reconstruct the ideal of chivalry
and catholicism as it was embodied in the chivalrous romances and other poems of those ages. It is this picturesqueness, this sharpness which makes Scott such a favourite with
artists. „His novels are a series of pictures", an English painter once said to me, „and it is hard to say whether he is greatest in landscape or history."

Yet, as I have said, Scott does not belong to our very
greatest poets. His characters are forcibly and truely drawn.
We know Marmion, Rebecca, Meg Merriles, and Domine
Samson as well as we know our everyday acquaintances, but
we know them no better. We should recognise them if we
met them in the streets, but we have not looked into their
hearts, we have not sat in judgement on their most secret
thoughts; we know what they are, but we do not know how
they became so. Who ever knew his dearest friend as well
as he knows Macbeth, Jago and Desdemona? Who ever looked so deeply into the heart of his sister, or his wife, as he
has into the hearts of Gretchen, Clärchen, and Otilia? The
characters of our nearest friends and relations are riddles to
us. In the works of the greatest artists the riddle is solved.
In those of Scott it is merely stated. He is a mighty, per-

haps the mightiest of magicians but he is no God.   He can
conjure up and command a thousand forms, but he cannot
create and reveal.   This is, I think, what Carlyle means
when he says that he paints his characters from without inwards, that he paints first the clothes, then the form, then
the manners, and last of all, or sometimes not at all, the
heart, that he makes the man to fit the clothes, instead of
the clothes to fit the man.

Closely connected with this weakness is his inability to
express passion.   He can describe it wonderfully, with a
truth, power and simplicity that have seldom been equaled,
but as soon as he must express it his power fails him.   Hence
his lyric poems, except when they are descriptive, are for
the most part, failures.   Some ballads in the old English
manner are dashed off with extraordinary force and spirit.
The Young Lochinvar has more of the character of our old
poetry than any other modern poem.   But as soon as he attempts a purely lyrical subject he gets beyond his depth.   In
short, Scott, though skilled beyond all his English contemporaries in dramatic effect, in the description of characters,
and in fertility of imagination, cannot claim the place, that
has too often been assigned him, among poets of the highest
rank.

Chapter III.

In our last chapter we had to do with the works of
Scott.   We found that they were distinguished by their great
power of painting the outside of life, but that he had not the
power of expressing deep passion.   His works are distinguished by variety, and dramatic arrangement, but he seldom, if ever, speaks words which go directly to the heart.
In these respects he is almost the exact opposite of Lord By-

ron. Indeed, it has been said, that the latter poet had all that Scott wanted, and wanted all that he possessed. Within certain bounds this is the case. They are the two poets of this age who had most immediate and universal success. I doubt whether they were the greatest poets of the period, but they certainly understood and embodied the spirit of their time better than any of their contemporaries. This is the reason why we have examined their works before those of the other poets of their age.

Byron was born in London on the 22nd of January 1788. Though descended of an ancient and noble house, he was not born to wealth. His father had been a spendthrift and was separated from his wife. Lady Byron had not more than £ 150 a year on which to live with her son. But this was not his only misfortune. He had been born lame, and much of his sensitiveness may be attributed to this defect. Nor was his mother qualified to educate such a son. Passionate and thoughtless, she alternately smothered him with caresses, and taunted him with his lameness. Before he was five years old he had learnt to wince under the taunt, and, to the end of his life, he could not bear to hear his deformity mentioned. At the death of his grand-uncle he succeeded to the title and estate of the family. He was then sent first to a private school, and afterwards to Harrow. But in his holidays he returned ever and again to Newstead-abbey, the house of his ancestors. This building made a deep impression on his mind, and long afterwards, when his boyish hopes had all been wrecked and he himself was exiled by public opinion from his native land, he dwelt lovingly on his old home.

Here the young poet loved to linger and to muse. Prevented by his lameness from mixing in the games of his schoolfellows, he became a thoughtful and rather dreamy boy; and Newstead-abbey was a place well fitted to dream in. Here too occured an event which, in his own opinion, made a deep impression on his life, and which was the subject of

some of his most beautiful poems. In 1803 he spent his va-
cation in the country. He was then 15 years old. Near
Newstead abbey was the estate of the Chaworths, and he
was a frequent guest at Annesley, their family-residence.
Though neighbours the families had not always been friends.
Indeed the last Lord Byron had killed the head of the Chaworths' house in a duel. Miss Chaworth, the daughter and
heiress of this gentleman, was the poets senior by about two
years. She was known in the whole country round for her
beauty. Byron saw and fell in love with her. He followed
her about wherever he could. She seems not to have dis-
liked her boy admirer, but then he was a b o y. She liked
him, played with him, chatted with him, and laughed at him.
Things went on in this way for a time, but they were des-
tined to come to a sad end. As he stood one evening beneath
her window, he heard her say to her maid-servant, who
had been teasing her about him. „Do you think I care
anything for that lame boy?" The speech, he said, was like
a shot through his heart; and long afterwards he wrote,
„Our union would have healed feuds in which blood had
been shed by our fathers, it would have joined lands broad
and rich, it would have joined at least one heart and two
persons not ill matched in years, and — and what has been
the result?" In his later years he looked back to the boyish
day-dream which was so cruelly dispelled as the turning point
of his life. I do not think that it was really so important
an event as he supposed it to be. He was too proud and
sensitive ever to have been a happy man. But when looking
back on the storms and troubles of a life that had not been
wisely spent, when reviewing the shipwrecked hopes of his
youth, and the feverish pleasures of his later years, it was
natural that he should love to dwell on that happy day-dream
of his boyhood, and sigh, if that had only ended otherwise
how different it all might have been.

In 1805 he left Harrow and entered Trinity college,

Cambridge. Two years later he published his first work:
„Hours of Idleness." This book is a collection of lyrical
poems. Taken as a whole, the verses are neither much better, nor much worse than those most boys write at that age.
The verse is not bad, but there is little or nothing of the
nervous force, which distinguished Byron's later poems, about
it. In the thought and feeling expressed there is little originality. The poems are, for the most part, common-place
imitations of older writers. Loch na Garr has it is true
kept its place in our memories, and deserves to do so, but
it owes much to the name of its author.

Spite the weakness and insignificance of these poems,
many traces of Byron's character are to be found in them.
He is here, as always, the hero of his verses. Every lyric
poet must of course write subjectively, he must speak in the
first person, and so on. Every real poet too, whether lyrical
or not, will often weave scenes and feelings from his own life
into his verse. His life is the material from which his poems
must be fashioned. He cannot be blamed for using this
material, as all poets before him have done, but then he
must remember that it is raw material. It is the ore which
contains the gold, not the gold itself. It must be purified
and refined in the fire of thought, before it really becomes
poetical. It is the thoughts and feelings of the poet, not his
person and circumstances, which should interest us. Part
of this Byron afterwards learnt. He learnt to distinguish the
poetical from the unpoetical, but he always remained the
hero of his verses, and in these, his earlier poems, he constantly reproduces thoroughly unpoetical incidents merely because they have a personal connexion with himself. He
gives us two rhymed histories of his family; he tells us how
he played, fought, and acted at school, and is careful to add
that he was applauded in Lear, and he does not smooth and
shape the scenes into form, or illumine them with a glow of
passion, as he did in after-life. He tells us all in a boast-

ful tone, and minutely, as if it must needs interest us. In short the „Hours of Idleness" is, as I have already said, as foolish and vain a series of poems, as most young men write — and publish, if they are unfortunate enough to have an opportunity. The book might have sunk quietly into oblivion, as most such books do, but, unfortunately, a copy fell into the hands of Lord Brougham. He seems to have been nettled by the arrogance of the preface, for he wrote a criticism of the work for the Edinburgh Review, to which he was then a contributor. The cristicism does not seem to me to have been unjust, but it was bitter, much bitterer than it would have been if undeserved. It cut Byron to the quick, and he resolved to be revenged, but he could not discover who was the author of the article in question. Some attributed it to Croker, some to Scott, some to other authors of the day. He did not however allow this difficulty to deter him. As he could not find out who his enemy was, he resolved to chastise every living author of note, of whose innocence he was not convinced. In this spirit „English bards and Scotch Reviewers" was written. This satire appeared in 1809. The most cursory glance shows the progress which Byron had made in two years. The verse is ringing, the style clear and sharp, the wit biting, and the tone that of a proud man justly angry, not that of a conceited boy wishing to show off. The poem deserves a high place in our satirical literature, and is likely to be remembered longer than many better works of the kind. It is the fate of most satires to be forgotten with the follies which they ridicule, and most follies pass quickly away to make room for new ones. The Dunciad, masterly as it is, is seldom read with pleasure in our own days, because we know but little of the miserable scribblers, whose absurdities Pope immortalized in it. But in „English Bards and Scotch Reviewers" Byron attacks men with whose works every educated man is familiar. Scott, Wordsworth, Coleridge, and other

poets, whose poems will be read as long as our language endures, are the heroes of his satire, and every point against them
tells as well to day as when the book was first published.
The strangest thing in the satire is, that in it Byron declared
himself an adherent of the classical school. We have already traced the struggle between it and a purer taste. At
the commencement of the 19th century it was all but dead
in poetry, but in criticism it still continued to exist. Now
it is not strange that Byron, when declaring war against all
living poets, should be glad to avail himself of the partisanship
of the classical writers. He was bound to them by a common
hatred. But it is strange that, when he had become recon-
ciled to his old enemies, when he had written works which
were moulded on the very principles which he had formerly
combatted, he should still continue to praise and defend the
very school to which he himself had given the death-blow.
Macaulay believes his admiration to have been sincere. He
thinks that through his whole life he broke the laws which
he himself believed to be just, from a love of praise. It may
have been so, but may we not in part attribute this contradiction between his works and his opinion to his pride? Is
it not possible that he may have been unwilling to declare
himself in the wrong, and still more unwilling to confess
that his admiration of Pope had never been genuine, and
that he therefore praised Pope and Dryden so loudly, that
he at last became a believer in his own praise.

English Bards and Scotch reviewers was a great success
for a young poet; yet it was, I think, unfortunate that he
published it. It devided him from the greatest of his contemporaries. It placed a great gulf between him and men
who could have helped and guided him. After its publication he stood alone, and though this position may have been
gratifying to his pride, it was in many ways injurious to
him. He himself confessed long afterwards, when he had be-

come the friend of many of those whom he had attacked, that it had been a thorn in his side ever since its publication.

During the years 1809, 1810, and 1811 he made a journey through Spain, Greece, and Turkey. The literary results of this journey were the two first Cantos of Childe Harold's Pilgrimage, and a series of lyrical verses which are now included in his Occasional Poems. The part of Childe Harold which he had already finished he published in 1812. Childe Harold, the hero of the poem, is a young, ill educated nobleman who, sated with the dissipations of England, sets out on his wanderings through the Continent. He is proud and gloomy, but gifted with an exquisite perception of the beauties of nature, and this poem consists of a series of his musings. The mountains and valleys of Spain with the muleteer singing as he passes slowly among them, the hills and plains of Greece with their thousand memories, the wide forests of Arcanania with the wild soldier groups reveling among them, and the deep blue sea — Byrons favourite theme, are all shortly and graphically painted, and over all is thrown, like the gloomy lurid light of an approaching thunderstorm, the melancholy pride of the hero and his dreary hopelessness. The rhythm which the poet chose is the Spenserian stanza, a form of verse excellently suited to the subject.

No poem of such force and originality had appeared in England since the death of Milton. It had an immense success and it deserved it. It was exactly suited to the spirit of the age. Of the gloomy melancholy which is common to it and all the other poems of its author, I intend to speak hereafter. We have now to do with the descriptions of scenery which occupy the greatest part of the poem. We shall see, when we come to the poetry of Wordsworth, Keats, and Shelley, that the commencement of the present century was marked by an intense enjoyment of the beauties of nature. Poets of all ages have loved woods and mountains, the bright flowers of spring and the deep tints of autumn, and they have introduced them into their poems. But our old poets used them as illustrations alone. They described ladies gathering flowers, but the flowers were only the ornaments of the lady; they told of dark forests and rocky hillsides, but these were only used as the background for their pictures of knights and magicians. But in the age of which we are now speaking nature was described for its own sake alone. Wordsworth introduced his characters very often merely to increase the charm of his landscapes.

Byron was not nearly so thoroughly acquainted with nature as Wordsworth. He could not paint the subtle ever changing beauty of natural landscapes with anything like the exactness of the lake-poet. But he made nature instinct with passion. He filled it with human emotions. He used it as a symbol of the soul. That is what makes „Childe Harolds Pilgrimage" so universally comprehensible, and bitterly as Byron hated Wordsworth, Macaulay is doubtless right in saying that he interpreted him to the people. The success of the poem was immediate, and, as he himself said, he awoke one morning and found himself famous.

Passing a few unimportant pieces we now come to his Eastern tales. These poems have much in common with the metrical romances of Scott. The form is nearly the same; though Byron's tales are shorter, and their rhythm more varied. Eastern life, with its gorgeous colouring and strange customs, was to Byron, what the history of the middle ages was to Scott. It was his peculiar province — the land of dark passion and mystery, in which every thing was possible. This series of tales began with the Giaour. It is a tale of love and wrong avenged by a deeper wrong. The scene is the Orient with its thousand strange and fantastic forms, with the mosque and the convent standing side by side, and peopled with monks and robbers, with lovely maidens and turbaned warriors, and amid them all moves the Giaour, with

his despairing frown and hopeless loneliness. The poem is
a series of fragments, now a burst of passion, and then a
description of scenery, or a hurried sketch of an event; yet
the impression made is deep and clear.

The Giaour was followed by a long series of tales of the
same class. These are the writings in which Byron approach-
eses Scott most nearly, yet here the difference between the
poets is most clearly marked. The Lady of the Lake and
Marmion attract us by the variety of their characters, and
the wildness of their adventures. These tales move us by the
depth of their passion. Scott delights in heroic acts, Byron
in fearful crimes. Scott was a masterly painter, he could
portray the outside of every character. Each of his persons
is individualised by a thousand little, but exact touches, each
apparently insignificant yet each important in its place. The
Highland Chieftain, and the Southern knight are distinguished by their very language. Byron had none of this power.
His poems are wild bursts of passion and dispair. His heroes
differ only in their circumstances, alter these, and the Corsair becomes the Giaour, and the Giaour the Corsair. But this
one character is drawn with masterly depth and power. He
is a strong, brave man, bound by no laws, but capable at
once of acts of astonishing generosity and of fearful crimes.
His heart is a volcano of passion, of undoubting inexhaus-
tible love and of implacable hatred. He scorns the world,
and is engaged in a ceaseless contest with it — a contest in
which he is forever vanquished. The heroines are fitting
companions for such men — women, capable of boundless,
passionate, unthinking love, but capable too of hatred as
passionate — maidens who will perish for their lovers without a sigh, but who have daggers hid beneath their robes
for the faithless lover, or the hated rival. Such characters are
doubtless unreal, but the passion they express is real. As
soon as Scott's heroes begin to express deep feeling they become common place, and we begin to doubt their sincerity;

as soon as Byron's characters speak of their love or hatred,
we forget that they are unnatural, we forget that the plot
is unreal, and we are carried away by their joy and anguish
— by their love and dispair. Byron wrote very quickly.
His tales are impassioned monologues. Their tone never al-
ters, except that the gloom deepens towards the end, while
Scott's tales are full of contrasts of light and shade. Scott
was in fact the story-teller, Byron the prophet.

These tales established their authors fame as a poet. He
was now the darling of English society. Men of all parties and creeds united in praising him. The highest ladies
in the land agreed in flattering him. Whatever he said
was admired, whatever he wrote was eagerly read. His
slightest acts were noted and imitated. Whatever he wore
became fashionable. He was a perfect gentleman, a light,
witty and agreeable companion, but the people of that age
saw more in him than that. They persisted in confounding him with his poetical creations. He was in their eyes
the Giaour, the Corsair and Childe Harold. They beheld
the man for whose sorrows they had wept living and moving before them, and they fell down at his feet and worshiped him. It it a pleasant thing to be worshiped, and
he assuméd the character they forced upon him. Nor was
this adoration confined to literary circles, or to the society
in which he was accustomed to move. In distant villages,
among the middle classes, and in religious families, where
poetry and fiction were in general forbidden, his poems
were to be found. Dissenting ministers who looked on
poetry as a sin prayed for him, as if he had been their
own son. Village maidens, who had seldom read any book
but the Bible, hid his verses under their pillows. The
wife of one clergyman of the church of England wrote a
prayer for him, which she repeated every morning and evening. In short, all England united in flattering and praising a young man of 26 years old. It is difficult for us to

understand this enthusiasm, but those who have read Byron's poetry when young can form at least some idea of it. Now that we can look at his character coolly, that we know his weakness, his littleness, and his vanity, we feel that such admiration was absurd. It was soon to come to an end. On the 2nd of January 1815 he married Miss Milbank. That was a blow to popular admiration. It robbed Byrons character of much of its romance. He had been looked upon as the hero of his own poems, and we must confess that it was rather strange that the Giaour should leave his cell and be married at church, in a common-place way, like other people. Had he committed a great and daring crime, it would not have been out of keeping with his imaginary character. But a common-place marriage was so unromantic that he could no more be looked upon as a noble, broken-hearted hero. The best that could be hoped from him was that he would become a good matter of fact husband. But even this was not to be. Byron could not have found a wife more unsuited to him than Miss Milbank. She was a well educated, but passionless woman, with no taste for poetry, but with some inclination to mathematical studies. Strict, exact, and highly respectable and methodical, she was the opposite of the poet in every respect. They quarrelled. Whose the fault was is not, and probably never will be known. Perhaps neither, perhaps both were to blame. At any rate the idol of the world was broken. Here was Conrad quarelling with Medora. Here was the poet who had been looked upon as the truest of lovers, and admired as such, illusing his wife, so that she was obliged to run away from him. The rage of the public was as extravagant as its worship had been. Before none had dared to whisper censure, now none dared to hint at excuse. The papers were filled with libels on the very man whom, a short time before, they had deified. Crowds collected to pelt him on his way to the house of Lords, and to hiss him at the theatre. Such was the state of public feeling, when,

on the 25th of April 1816 he left England forever. He had
one child by this marriage, a daughter — Agusta Ada. Byron seems to have felt the separation acutely, though he had
not lived happily with his wife.

We must now turn to the lyrical poems which Byron
wrote about this time. The first that demand our attention
are the Hebrew Melodies, which were published before his
marriage. The old Testament had always been one of his
favourite books, and we find traces of its influence in many
of his .poems. At the request of a friend he consented to
write the words for a series of Hebrew melodies which were
then to be published.. The subjects are passages of the Bible
and laments over the fallen glory of Zion.

The political events of 1813, 1814 and 1815 could not
fail to attract the attention of Byron. The character and fate
of Napoleon exerted a great influence over his imagination.
He was too largehearted to be blinded by a national preju-
dice. He sympathized with the fall of the hero; he partook
of the grief of the French. These feelings produced a series
of poems. The first of these was the „Ode to Napoleon Buo-
naparte", which was written on April the 10th 1814. It was
a burst of bitter sarcasm, an outbreak of passionate anger.
But such anger and sarcasm are evidently, to use the words
of one of our modern poets, „only love turned inside out".
Napoleon had abdicated. The high hopes of his followers
were all wrecked. The man who had sat in judgement upon
kings had bent to the sentence of his enemies. It was a sad
sight to those who had worshiped this man, an unheroic
end to the great tragedy, had it been indeed the end.

„The desolator desolate!
The victor overthrown!
The arbiter of others' fate
A suppliant for his own.
Is it some yet imperial hope
That with such change can calmly cope,

Or dread of death alone?
To die a prince, or live a slave,
Thy choice is most ignobly brave.

Who does not feel that such lines as these are the expression of a disappointed hope, of reverence for an object
that has proved itself unworthy of reverence? Napoleon returned from Elba, and in all the crowds that thronged to
meet him, there was no heart that was filled with a wilder
exstacy of gladness than Byron's. Then came Waterloo, when
the last hope of France was trodden down beneath the feet
of the united kings of Europe; then the dark days of dispair, the capture and imprisonment of Napoleon and the
murder of Ney. Byron embodied many of the sad feelings
of those days in poems.

Nowhere is the contrast between the characters of
Scott and Byron more clearly marked than in their treatment
of Napoleon. Scott could see in him nothing but a tyrant
and an enemy. He looked at him from the national point
of view. Byron saw that both his fate and character were
colossal, that he had to do with one who could not be judged
by common standards — with a man whose work, both for
good and evil, had been gigantic. He looked at him from a
poetical point of view. Scott was the poet of the past,
Byron the exponent of the future. He had none of that nar-
row-minded patriotism which is so often praised as a virtue.
The picture of the hero on the lonely rock, of the gigantic genius bound by pigmies, of the conqueror of Europe
dying broken-hearted and in exile, was too like the dark
creations of his own imagination not to affect him deeply.
But it was not the tragic fate of Napoleon alone, that excited
his admiration He believed that the people would gain nothing by Waterloo. He felt that the one great ruler would
be replaced by a hundred petty tyrants, that the blood, which
the nations had sown so plentifully at Leipzig and Waterloo,
would bring forth no fruit, and a deeper and higher feeling

was mingled with the pity and the terror, which the great tragedy of 1815 could not fail to excite. He mourned not only over the banished hero and enslaved France, he grieved that the revolution was conquered. While Scott saw nothing but the blaze of bonfires and the pomp of victory, Byron saw that mankind had gained little by the fall of Napoleon. Hence the one poet wrote a life of Napoleon, that was so superficial that it may almost be called a caricature, while the other composed songs in his honour which have seldom been surpassed even by French poets.

CHAPTER IV.

It had been hard for Byron to be cast down from the high place he had occupied. Praise was more than usually sweet, blame more than usually bitter to his excitable, sensitive, and vain nature. The time that passed between his separation from his wife and his departure from England was doubtless one of keen mental anguish. But this sorrow exercised a purifying and deepening influence on his poetry. He had coquetted with grief and dispair before, but he had worn his melancholy as a „dark mask in the carnival of the world." Now his disguise had become too real. Every hope was blighted, and, even if it were by his own fault, that would not make it less bitter. He was parted from his wife and child, he was excluded from the society which he had ruled, the doors of advancement in the state were closed against him, and he was exiled, by public opinion, from his native land. The first poetical products of this state of mind were the poems which are printed in his works under the title of Domestic pieces. In these we find a depth, a truth and power, for which we should seek in vain in his earlier verses. The words seem to come directly from his

heart. They are the poets protest against the injustice of
the world, yet ever and anon the sad confession is repeated

„I have been cunning in mine overthrow
The careful pilot of my proper woe.“

These are, I believe, the sincerest poems Byron ever
wrote, but they fell upon estranged ears. The people who
had caught at his slightest verses and had found romance
in his slightest movements, refused to believe his confession. Formerly they had persisted in accepting each of
his poetical creations as a picture of himself, now they refused to believe him when he opened up to them the very
depths of his heart.

On leaving England, Lord Byron proceeded up the
Rhine, to Switzerland, and thence to Italy. On the way
he completed the third Canto of Child Harold. Here his genius for the first time appeared in its full power, but we will
leave it till the conclusion of the fourth Canto, when we shall
be able to consider the work as a whole. We cannot pause
to examine all the smaller poems which he wrote in 1816,
but the Dream is to important to be passed by without a
word. It is the story of the poets life in a series of pictures.
As he looked back on the past, with its wasted powers and
wrecked hopes, the face of his first love, Mary Chaworth,
rose before him. In the days of his fame and happiness she
had been all but forgotten. We find no trace of her existence in the poems which he published between the Hours
of Idleness and his separation from Lady Byron. But now
that his heart was softened by sorrow, the hours of his boyhood seemed very bright and joyous, and all that had passed
since very gloomy and drear. Since then his life had been
a feverish struggle, a weary wandering, and it now seemed
to him as if that had all come because Mary Chaworth had
not loved him. The struggle and the wanderings, his ill
fated marriage, and indeed the whole past seemed to him
to have been nothing but a vain attempt to forget her. Such

is the tale of the dream . The plan is masterly. It is introduced by a few lines on sleep and dream-life, which are
among the finest that ever fell from his pen. Then the Dream
itself begins. The first scene is a hill near Newstead Abbey,
though the name is not mentioned, and below lies a beautiful English scene.

> „These two, a maiden and a youth, were there
> Gazing — the one on all that was beneath
> Fair as herself — but the boy gazed on her;
> And both were young, and one was beautiful."

Then the love of the boy is described in a few delicate
and forcible lines, but

> „she loved another,
> And on the summit of that hill she stood
> Looking afar, if yet her lovers steed
> Kept pace with her expectancy, and flew."

Then we have the parting of the lovers in an „antique
Oratory", in which the suppressed passion of the youth is
painted with wonderful force and delicacy. Afterwards we
see him on his wanderings through the East, and we
feel that he is wandering only that he may forget that old
love of his. Again the dream is changed, and „she is wed
to one who did not love her better" and children play around
her knees, and yet she is not happy.

> „A change came o'er the spirit of my dream.
> The wanderer was return'd. — I saw him stand
> Before an Altar — with a gentle bride;
> Her face was fair, but was not that which made
> The Starlight of his Boyhood; — as he stood
> Even at the altar, o'er his brow there came
> The self same aspect, and the quivering shock
> Which in the antique Oratory shook
> His bosom in its solitude; and then —
> As in that hour — a moment o'er his face
> The tablet of unutterable thoughts

Was traced, — and then it faded, as it came,
And he stood calm and quiet, and he spoke
The fitting vows, but heard not his own words,
And all things reel'd around him; he could see
Not that which was, nor that which should have been —
But the old mansion, and the accustom'd hall,
And the remember'd chambers, and the place,
The day, the hour, the sunshine; and the shade,
All things pertaining to that place and hour,
And her who was his destiny, came back
And thrust themselves between him and the light:
What business had they there at such a time?"

Then again the scene is changed, and we behold the
lady of his love plunged in madness, and the youth at war
with his kind, hating, and hated by them.

„My dream was past, it had no further change.
It was of a strange order, that the doom
Of these two creatures should be thus traced out
Almost to a reality — the one   -
To end in madness — both in misery."

Such is the dream, which seems to me the most perfect
of Byron's poems. In other of his works he doubtless shows
a greater command over language, and a vaster range of genius, but none of them seize the imagination so forcibly as
this, none have such unity of design, such finish of execution. It is too an important moment in the life of Byron;
after writing it he seldom or ever refered to Lady Byron, in
his poetry, as having had an important influence on his life.
In fact he treated his marriage, in his later writings, as an
unfortunate attempt to banish the memory of the sweet girlish face, „which made the starlight of his boyhood." „I've
tried another's fetters too", he exclaims

„With charms perchance as fair to view,
And I would fain have loved as well;
But some unconquerable spell

Forbade my bleeding breast to own
A kindred care for aught save one."

His next great work was Manfred. This dramatic poem
was commenced in 1816, and finished in 1817. It was Byron's first attempt at dramatic composition. The plot, if
Manfred can be said to have any plot, is very simple. The
hero oppressed by a deep sorrow, and the remembrance of
a mysterious crime appeals to the spirits of Earth, Air, and
Ocean for forgetfulness, in vain. He then penetrates into
the hall of Arimanes, where he meets the spirit of Astarte —
his former love, who fortells his death.. Finally the Abbot
of St. Maurice visits him, and exhorts him to repent, but is
unsuccessful, an evil spirit then rises and claims Manfred's
soul, but he braves it, and the evil spirit retires; on this
Manfred dies. Even this slight sketch is sufficient to show
that the dramatical element is entirely wanting in the poem.
There is no action, there are no characters in the piece. It
is so to speak a series of episodes. The last scene must of
course come at the end, because the hero dies in it, but the
position of almost any of the other scenes might be changed
without diminishing the effect. The inferior characters come
and go without making much impression on the reader, or
doing much to help the plot forwards. The Abbot is the
best of them, but, how little depends upon him, is proved by
the fact that in the first draft of the piece he was a diaboli-
cally wicked wretch, while in the poem, as it now stands,
he is a saint. Even the external dramatic form is not sustain-
ed. Manfred is a series of monologues. The hero muses instead of acting. In his tower, on the cliffs of the Jungfrau,
and in the hall of Arimanes he does nothing but expatiate on
his greatness and his wretchedness. His character is, it is
true, powerfully drawn, but it is not dramatically developed.
It is from his soliloquies, and not from his actions, that we
learn that he is great, proud, and unhappy. In short, the
whole treatment is essentially undramatic; but then Byron

did not intend to write a drama. He says that he has endeavoured to render it „quite impossible to produce it on the
stage". As a poem then it must be judged, and we must
confess that it contains several passages in the poets best
style. Such is the scene in which Manfred meets the spirit of
Astarte, and the description of the Coliseum by moonlight.
Yet we cannot but wonder at the enthusiasm with which
this work was hailed at its publication. The unvarying wretchedness of the hero is monotonous, and it wearies rather
than interests us Besides the impression is weakened by its
frequent repetition. Manfred is only Child Harold in a new
position. The other dramatic works of Byron have the same
faults as Manfred, and are less powerful than it. There is
but one exception, Heaven and Earth. The rest we may
pass without farther notice, but on this poem we must linger
a few moments. It is in many respects one of the finest of
Byrons works. It has more unity, interest and finish than
any of his other dramatical essays. He called it a mystery,
not because there is any thing particularly mysterious in the
plot, but because, like the old plays of that name, it is tak-
en from the biblical narrative. The passage on which it is
founded is the following extract from the book of Genesis.
„And it came to pass that the sons of God saw the daughters
of men that they were fair; and they took them wives of all
which they chose . . . . And there were giants on the earth
in those days . . . . And God saw that the wickedness of man
was great in the earth, and that every imagination of the
thoughts of his heart was only evil continually . . . . And
the Lord said, I will destroy man whom I have created from
the face of Earth". A grander subject can scarcely be conceived, and Byron's genius was well fitted to treat it. Here
was colossal passion, a fearful fate, and an age where imagination could run riot without passing the bounds of probability. What cannot be believed of a time when the Earth
blossomed in her primeval beauty, when the fiery sword of

the Archangel might still be seen guarding the paths that led
to the tree of life, and when the very sons of God descended
from the regions of the blest to hold converse with the daughters of men. The whole subject is placed before us in all
its grandeur. In the very first scene Anah and Aholibahmah, two sisters of the daughters of Cain, leave their fathers' tents at the dead of night, to invoke their Angel lovers,
and the tragic interest of the story goes on deepening to the
moment when „the windows of heaven are opened, and the
fountains of the great deep are broken up", and all created life,
save the little remnant of Seth's seed, is overthrown in the
universal destruction. The characters too, though they are
for the most part only sketched, are better conceived than in
any other of Lord Byron's dramas. Anah, the younger of the
sisters, is an embodiment of sincere self forgetting love. She
is religious too, bowing with resignation to the will of God,
and fearful of disobeying his commands. Aholibahmah on
the other hand is well fitted to be a Seraph's bride. She feels
that in love she is equal to him, that his love has raised her
above the rest of the daughters of men. Their characters are
finely contrasted even at their first entrance. Anah says
„But, Aholibahmah,
I love our God less, since his angel loved me;
This cannot be of good; and though I know not
That I do wrong, I feel a thousand fears
That are not ominous of right.
And her sister proudly answers
               Then wed thee
Unto some son of clay, and toil and spin!
   * * * * * * * * * * *
Marry and bring forth dust.
   So in their invocation Anah prays, Aholibahmah almost
commands her lover to descend; and when Japhet would fain
save them from the approaching destruction, she taunts him

with his descent from Seth, and boasts that the first murderer was her forefather.

> And doest thou think that we ,
> With Cain's, the eldest born of Adam's, blood
> Warm in our veins, would mingle with Seth's children?

And again: He was our father's father;

> The eldest born of man, the strongest, bravest
> And most enduring : — Shall I blush for him,
> From whom I had my being? Look upon
> Our race; behold their stature and their beauty.

And again: Must we

> Cling to a son of Noah for our lives?

Yet in the fearful hour of destruction, it is she who bids
her lover return to heaven and leave her to her fate, while
her sister still clings to Azaziel for protection, and can
hardly bring herself to give up his love. The angels say
and do but little, they would be lay figures but for their
resolution to forfeit heaven rather than desert their human
brides. Japhet is the hero of the piece. He is in love with
Anah, and would gladly save her even at the cost of his
own life. But he grieves not over her alone, but over the
whole lovely earth. At times he almost questions the justice
of God, at others he defends it against all accusation. But
in all moods, he shrinks with horror from the fearful loneliness of the new world. „Why“, he exclaims at the end of
the drama, amid all the horrors of the new chaos, „Why, when
all perish, why must I remain?“ Noah is a thorough contrast to his son, cold and passionless, he reminds us often
of the puritans, by the calmness with which he looks on the
destruction of the world. When Japhet in a passion of anguish beseeches God, even now, in the last hour, to spare
the doomed creation he calmly says

> „Wouldst thou have God commit a sin for thee?
> Such would it be

To alter his intent
For a mere mortal sorrow.

Heaven and Earth as we have it is only a fragment. It was
not very favourably received by the public, so Byron never
finished it. From the first part it is difficult to guess at what
the second might have been. It would probably have followed the fates of Anah and Aholibahmah, who are carried
away by their Angel lords at the conclusion of the play as
it now stands. The key to the whole plan is I think contained in the following passages.

The first is from Aholibahmah's invocation.

     — There is a ray
In me, which, though forbidden yet to shine,
I feel was lighted at thy God's and thine.
It may be hidden long: death and decay
Our mother Eve bequeathed us — but my heart
Defies it: though this life must pass away,
Is that a cause for thee and me to part?
Thou art immortal — so am I: I feel —
  I feel my immortality o'ersweep
All pains, all tears, all time, all fears, and peal,
Like the eternal thunders of the deep,
Into my ears this truth — „Thou liv'st forever!"
  But if it be in joy
I know not, nor would know;
That secret rests with the Almighty giver
Who folds in clouds the fonts of bliss and woe.
  But thee and me He never can destroy;
Change us He may, but not o'erwhelm; we are
Of as eternal essence, and must war
With Him, if He will war with us: with thee
I can share all things, even immortal sorrow;
  For thou hast ventured to share life with me.

The second is Japhet's answer to the spirits.

  The eternal will

Shall deign to expound this troubled dream
Of good and evil; and redeem
   Unto Himself all times, all things;
And, gathered under his almighty wings,
   Abolish hell!
And to the expiated Earth
Restore the beauty of her birth,
Her Eden in an endless paradise,
Where man no more can fall as once he fell,
And even the very demons shall do well!
S p i r i t s. And when shall take effect this wondrous spell?
J a p h e t. When the Redeemer cometh; first in pain
   And then in glory.

No one can read the sad story of Byrons life in Italy
without profound sorrow. It is the story of talents wasted, and
genius misapplied. He resided for a long time at Venice where
he plunged into the lowest depths of disoluteness. Maddened
by the injustice with which he had been treated, he sought
forgetfulness in wine. The young English nobleman, who
had lately been the Idol of London society, now mixed with
the lowest of the low. The poet, whose impassioned words
still moved all hearts, revelled in the most tasteless excesses.
By degrees this evil life began to tell upon his health, and it
almost seemed as if the end of the poet were to be low indeed.
He was rescued from it by a connection which, though in
itself culpable, seemed pure to the society mid whom he lived.

The few important works of his which remain to be noticed we must now shortly review. They are the last two
cantos of Childe Harold, the Vision of Judgement, and Don
Juan. When we pass from the second to the third canto of
Childe Harold, we are struck at once by the difference between the two. The first is a series of fine descriptions, tinged
by melancholy, the last a passionate outburst of anguish.
The woe no longer colours the descriptions, it penetrates
them, and uses all nature as a mere picture of itself. Harold's

name is still used in the third Canto, but it has ceased to be even an attempt at a character, it is merely another name for Byron. The poet describes his own sorrows, and his own fate, and sometimes in words that we cannot but feel are sincere. But it is not only in depth of feeling, and force of expression that the last part of this poem is superior to the first. The descriptive pieces are written with a liveliness and power which it would be difficult to find elsewhere.

The Vision of Judgement is a very different poem. On the death of George the third, Southey, the poet laureate, wrote a vision of Judgement in hexameters. In it he told how the king had ascended to heaven, and been received there, with a series of compliments, such as those with which earthly courtiers are accustomed to greet their sovereigns. The whole thing was as absurd as bad taste could make it. George the third was a much better man than most princes are, but he was a much worse king. His stupidity was almost incredible, and his obstinacy was almost greater than his stupidity. He did all in his power to ruin England, and to overthrow the constitution. He was unsuccessful, it is true, and there can be no doubt he was a good husband and father, still he was hardly fitting subject for celestial praise. Byron at once saw the whole absurdity of the situation; hence his Vision of Judgement, a parody on that of Southey. This is one of the bitterest satires of the age. Hatred, scorn, and wit are united in a marvellous degree. Finally, it is true, King George is left in heaven, but he slips in through the back door, in the midst of the confusion occasioned by Southey, commencing one of his poems.

And when the tumult dwindled to a calm,
I left him, practising the hundredth Psalm

We now come to Don Juan, the last, and in some respects the greatest of Lord Byron's works. In it he commenced an entirely new style, unless we like to consider Beppo as its forerunner. It is a wild story, told in a light gossiping style. Goethe wrote thus of it:

„Don Juan is a work of boundless genius, misanthropic to the bitterest cruelty, philanthropic to the depths of the sweetest sympathy, and as we know and respect the author, and have made up our minds not to wish him other than he is, we enjoy thankfully what he offers us with such lavish freedom, and even licence. The strange, wild, inconsiderate contents of the poem is suited to the technical treatment of the verse."

The poem treats of every thing, from the dispair of disappointed love, to the best way of curing a headache. On one page we find a rhymed criticism on modern poetry, on the next an account of a shipwreck, and on a third a violent attack on the ministry. Here, for the first time, we find the style of writing which Heine afterwards appropriated and used with such power that it has since been called by his name. „The poet raises us to the highest summits of romantic enthusiasm, only to dash us more cruelly against the rocks of reality". But this is not, I think, to be attributed to frivolity. It is in keeping with the conversational tone of the poem. In society, when a subject becomes painfully serious, we end the discussion by a joke. That is just what Byron does in Don Juan. With a light word he quits a subject that is getting too serious for the nature of the poem. The book is a delightful bit of gossip upon things in general, loosely held together by the thread of the story. It has been much blamed for its immorality, and we must confess that, when placed by the side of Marmion or the Excursion, it is loose; but it is not more so than many classical works are. The tone too, though far from pure, is much more healthy than that of most of his earlier poems. But what we most admire in Don Juan is the poets mastery over the English language. Their is no single poem in the whole range of our literature in which its various capabilities are exhibited in an equal degree. H. von Treitschke in his masterly essay on „Lord Byron and Radicalism" gives it the highest place among all the poet's works, and it certainly is the one in which his various powers come most fully into play. The latter Cantos are however inferior to the earlier.

Such was the work with which Lord Byron was busied when the news reached him that the Greeks had recommenced their long struggle with the Turks. He had ever been an ardent lover of liberty, and he had assisted the Italian patriots by contributions of large sums of money. To Greece he was bound by a thousand ties. It had been to him what Italy is to most artists. It was the land in which his character and genius had ripened. There he had written a great part of the poem on which his fame was founded. There too he had laid the scene of many of his earlier romances, and his imagination still loved to linger amid the hills and valleys which are hallowed by so many sacred memories. Accordingly he resolved to go in person to take part in the great struggle in which the Greeks were engaged. He arrived on the 5th of January 1824, and was received with the greatest enthusiasm by the patriots. The vigour of his movements there proved him to be possessed of powers which he had never before exhibited. But his constitution was worn out by the sorrows and excesses of his latter years. It was evident that he could not live long, and he himself only wished to die on the field of battle. But this was not to be. On the 19th of April 1824 he died of a fever brought on by a cold. The last act of his life, says a French poet, was the noblest of his poems.

Byron cannot be judged alone, nor can we understand his genius thoroughly, if we compare him with English writers only. His works were but a link in a great chain of literary productions. He belonged to the school which was commenced by the Nouvelle Heloïse and the Confessions, which then produced Werther and the Robbers and whose last great productions were the works of Heine. He had some qualities in common with each of these authors. He had the gloomy egotism of Rousseau, the love of nature which

Goethe displayed in Werther, the love of savage daring which
Schiller embodied in Carl Moor, and in his latter days some
of the wit and irony of Heine. The moral teaching of this
school, as far as they can be said to have had any, was that
man is born to wretchedness, and that the best thing he can
do is either to plunge into fearful crime, or sit down and
alternately laugh and cry over his misery, that virtue and
duty have no existence, and that all great men must necessarily be at war with society. In short their system was the
negation of all that men had been used to reverence. Of
this gospel Byron's works are the greatest embodiment. I do
not of course mean that he was the greatest of the writers
I have just mentioned, far from it, Roussau is the only one
of them who stood below him; but he was more entirely possessed of the spirit of the school than either of the others.
His works are, with the exception of Don Juan, one unbrok-
en cry of anguish. The form is, altered, but the subject is
ever the same, it is his own greatness and his own misery.
Much of the popularity of his poetry is attributable to its
egotistical and melancholy tone. It is difficult for us to understand how this could be the case. Few grown up people
in our own days can, I fancy, really enjoy the Robbers or
the Sorrows of Werther, still fewer can sympathise with the
sorrows of Rousseau, and if Heine's works are still read, it is
in spite rather than because of the melancholy, scornful tone
of some of them. To us the Confessions seem a record of
troubles which were either imaginary or well deserved.
Their author, even by the testimony of his own works, seems
to us a weak and foolish man. To his contemporaries he
seemed a hero, and a saint. Schiller gave expression to the
feelings of his own age, when he compared him to Socrates.
By many he was placed beside our Saviour in moral purity.
The same is true of Byron. When we compare his works
and life, we feel that he had known great sorrows, but we
feel also that much of the misery he boasts of is mere affec-

tation. We know that, while he proclaimed aloud that the
praise and blame of the world was nothing to him, the re-
-mark of an anonymous writer on his lameness maddened him.
We know that, while he was writing poems to Mary Chaworth
in which he attributed all the misfortunes of his life to his
love for her, he was passionately attached to another woman.
We know that spite of his declaration that
„Few who dwell beneath the sun,
Have loved so long and loved but one,"
he was one of the most fickle and inconstant of lovers. But
his contemporaries did not know all this. They believed he
was the gloomy heroic being he represented himself to be,
and they admired him. It is easy to ridicule such admiration,
to show how much weakness lay in the pretended strength,
but the time is past when such ridicule is needed. A few
clever boys, it is true, still look upon his heroes as the models of all true greatness, and practise before their looking —
glasses a Byronic sneer, but this admiration passes away
with the other follies of boyhood. With these the critic has
nothing to do. It is useless to ridicule a folly that has passed away. But we may well ask, whence came the false taste
that was once so general, and how was it that such men as
Goethe, Schiller and Byron should have been affected by it?
Every healthy literature is the expression of the wants
and longings of its own age. It is the embodiment of its
ideal, or at worst of its search after an ideal. It gives a
voice to the dumb yearnings of the national heart. Some
times the works of a single poet do this. Shakespeare is such
a representative of England in the Elizabethan age. All
that was highest and best in our country, at that time, is
to be found mirrored in his works. But oftener a number
of poets are needed. Each mirrors a single side of the national life. Each speaks to a sect or party, and gives them
what they want. He speaks not for himself alone but for
them. Such was our literature at the commencement of the

present century. During the latter half of the seventeenth
and the commencement of the eighteenth century, on the
other hand, no nation in Europe had a really national literature. The poetry of France, great as it was, was court-
poetry. That of Germany and England was a mere imitation of that of France. Hence the feelings, which were
embodied in the writings of Byron and the other poets
whom we have classed with him, may have slumbered
long in the hearts of the people without finding an outlet.
That it was so we have clear proof. Before Rousseau published the first of his works, suicide had raged like a mania
in France. Young men shot themselves, leaving letters
behind them to say that they had done so not because of
any particular misfortune, but because life did not seem
worth the having. In Germany Werther was written after
Goethe and several of his friends had passed through the
state of mind which the book describes, and, though the
work itself may be slightly coloured by the study of Rousseau, we cannot attribute the whole state of feeling that
caused it to the influence of a French author. Indeed I believe that his influence on the book itself is greatly over-
rated. From this, I think, it is pretty clear that the works
were the symptoms, and not the cause, of a deep seated
disease. Indeed the influence of books is as a rule greatly
overvalued. People are not made religious or irreligious, virtuous or vicious by the books they read; they choose their
reading according to their character. But whence came this
deep feeling of restless discontent, this morbid disgust of
life? That is the question we have now to answer. The
history of the world proves that it is impossible to do away
with the ideal part of man's nature. If it is not allowed to
develop itself healthily it makes itself felt as a disease. If
religion be repressed it only makes way for superstition.
The age which preceded the revolution offers a thousand
proofs of this. The philosophers declared, there was no God.

The men of science showed that there was no room left for the soul in the universe, and the wits ridiculed in no measured terms the absurdity of the doctrines in which their parents had believed. Never was there to be found a more enlightened and less prejudiced society than that of Paris at that period. Yet it was in freethinking, sceptical Paris that every new superstition found eager votaries. The age of Voltaire and Diderot was also the age of Mesmer and Cagliostro. The same people who believed in „The System of nature". thronged the halls where, in the garb of an oriental priest, the cunningest of modern impostors taught a system in comparison with which the rudest superstitions of the middle ages appear wise and beautiful. It is useless to multiply examples. The fact, however it may be explained away, is, I believe, universally acknowledged.

Now when we compare the state of society in the middle ages with that of modern times we find that much of its vast progress must be attributed to the division of labour. By the application of this principle much more can be produced, by a given amount of labour, than in any other way. But I doubt if the system is as beneficial to each individual labourer as is generally supposed. In the middle ages the retainer of a Baron led a life of never ending variety. One day he was tilling the ground, the next he was following his lord to battle, or helping to repair his castle. The farming, fighting, and building were all no doubt badly done, but all the different talents of the man were called into play. In our days such a life is impossible. One man spends the whole of his life in making pins' heads, another in adding up accounts, a third in copying letters. Each of these things is better done by the modern plan, but the workmen, in their hours of business, have ceased to be men, and have become mere parts of a huge machine. All that is highest and best in their nature is utterly useless, but it is not — it cannot be — utterly destroyed. It seeks a vent for itself. It be-

comes sometimes a curse instead of a blessing. Hence the
brutal immorality of our great towns. Hence, too, the fa-
naticism of our religious sects, the spread of Mormonism and
many of the most appaling phenomena of our age. To the
same class I believe the „Welt-Schmerz" which is embodied
in Byron's poetry belongs. A clever boy comes from school,
full of high hopes and aspirations, and he is apprenticed to
a dry mechanical business. He feels that here there is no
room for his character to develop itself. He discovers that
his hopes have been mere dreams. The very ends for which
he is to work seem mean and low to him, all life appears
nothing but an unweeded garden. Man delights him not
nor woman neither. The nobler his nature the more glaring is the contrast between it and his circumstances; the
deeper his intellectual interests the greater the gulf which
is fixed between his ideal and his real life. He feels that
no one understands him, that he cannot comprehend his
own yearnings. He nurses his melancholy. He wears it as
a badge to distinguish him from the unthinking herd. To
such a youth Byron speaks as a prophet. His poems are
the expression of the thoughts and feelings for which he
could find no words. His heroes are at war with the society which he hates. Their very crimes seem nobler to
him than the selfish morality of the counting-house. To
him Werther, Carl Moor and Manfred seem martyrs for the
truth that the soul is more than the body. Such a state of
mind is now only a transition state, a kind of „mental mea-
sles", which most clever boys pass through, but the time was
when the whole intellectual society of Europe was infected
with it. It was the age of Werther, the Robbers, and Byron.

If we examine Lord Byrons works critically, we shall
find that, spite his extraordinary power, we cannot award him
any more than Scott a place among poets of the very highest rank. In Shakspeare's works we find characters truer
than those of Scott, and passion truer than that of Byron.

It is so with all poets of the very first order. They draw a character which is individualized in the highest degree, a man as distinct as those we meet daily, as clearly distinguish-ed from every other, as each man is from his fellows. Then they reveal the inmost recesses of his heart. They let him speak of his love and sorrow, of his joy and woe. Take Lear. What passage in Byron's works can be compared in passion with the best scenes in that fearful tragedy? What words of his touch the heart like those of the mad old king? Yet who ever thought of confounding Shakespeare with Lear? He stands before us a distinct personality, a clearly objective fi-gure, no poet in disguise. It is only poets of the very grea-test genius that can thus unite passion with characteristic. Poets of less power fall for the most part into two great classes. The first of these draw characters. They observe closely and copy nature. They draw men who have a strong appearance of reality, and who are clearly distinguished from each other. Their characters act and speak naturally. But they can go no farther. They cannot reveal the secret springs of their actions. They cannot stir the heart with pas-sion, because they cannot identify themselves with their he-roes. The second class consists of subjective poets. Their power begins where that of the first class ceases. They speak from the heart. Their poems are bursts of passion. Their characters are only a series of emotions. They have no reality, no individuality. They are at best but the masks which con-ceal the features of the poet — the vessels from which his emotions are poured. Scott belongs to the first, Byron to the second class. It follows, as a matter of course, that Scott's range is wider while Byron's poetry is deeper. The outside of life is the province of the one, the heart that of the other poet. It need not therefore surprise us that Scott was more easily dazzled than this great contempo-rary by the pomp of the tournament, and the circumstance of battle, that he delighted in vivid contrasts of light and

shade, or that these contrasts are for the most part external.
It was his nature to do so; just as it was the nature of Byron to seize at once the heart of the matter.   When they
treat the same subject, the difference of their talents becomes
at once evident.   The song of the Hebrew maid in Iven-
hoe is well known.   In it Scott has selected all that is most
picturesque in the history and belief of Israel.   It would be
difficult to find a poem, of equal length, in which the wondrous story of that fated race is painted with equal taste and
discernment.   Yet when we compare it with the Hebrew melodies it seems cold and shallow.

It was this power of looking below the surface that led
Byron into his worst fault — a love of moral paradox.   Much
of Scott's moral heathiness must be attributed to the fact
that he dealt with the outside of life alone.   He believed
that men and things are nearly what they seem.   He did not
trouble himself with the springs of thought and feeling, he
cared for actions alone; and these are easily divided into bad
and good.   Byron looked deeper.   He saw that good feelings, ill directed, may lead to crimes, that the words and
deeds of a man are but faint, and often false pictures of his
character, that the laws that bind the world are not always
just, that the opinions of men are not always the highest
court of appeal.   He told wild tales of exceptional characters.
They were received with rapture.   He painted strange mix-
tures of good and evil.   They were applauded.   So he went
on, until at last he began to believe and teach that the
laws of society are always unjust, the opinions of mankind
always wrong.   This may justly be regretted and blamed, but
it would be unjust not to remember when reviewing his poems
and his character, that the worst errors of his works arose
from an endeavour to comprehend the mysterious nature of
man, and that the last act of his wayward and all but wasted
life was truly disinterested and noble.

Thomas Moore was a light, versatile writer, gifted with

a sharp wit and lively fancy, but with no very great imaginative power. His earlier works, though they were well
received at the time of their publication, are now but little
read. His satires however have a more permanent value.
They have none of the broad humour of Hudibras, none of the
epigrammatic point of Pope, none of the bitterness of Byron.
They seem to be the products of high spirits rather than of
hatred. Their wit is that of a man of the world. It does
not cut deep, indeed it hardly stings. It aims rather at making the hearer laugh, than at making its subject miserable.
In short, it is the wit of the drawing-room, not that which
is generally to be found in satire. These poems are all lightly
and gracefully written, and there are passages in them which
are exceedingly comic. The most celebrated is the „Fudge
family in Paris".

The narrative poems of Moore resemble, in some respects, those of Scott and Byron. They have the same form
of verse, and nearly the same tone; but they want the plastic power of the one poet, and the deep passion of the other.
Their principal charms are the melody of their rhythm, and
the richness of their imagery. The customs and poetry of
Persia were Moores favourite subjects. They were to him
what Scotch history was to Scott, and Turkish life to Byron;
but his pictures have much less truth and power than those
of his great contemporaries. His characters are English men
and women in Persian masks. His tales are graceful romances, but they never make any deep impression. Lalla Rookh
is the most celebrated of them. It is a series of four poems,
loosely connected by a prose tale. It was at one time very
popular, and it may still be read with pleasure. The Loves
of the angels was far less successful. The subject was beyond
his power. His angels are not angels, nor are they men and
women, they are gentlemen and ladies, and we must confess
that the ladies are blue-stockings, and even the gentlemen

rather inclined to be pedantic. Yet it contains some passages
in his best manner.

It is however on his songs that Moore's fame will rest.
He was the greatest lyrical poet of his age, and his Irish
melodies will be remembered long after all the rest of his
poems are forgotten. They are not wild bursts of passion
like Byron's shorter poems. They resemble the amatory poetry
of the middle ages rather than any modern poet with whom
I am acquainted. His verses are fanciful and musical rather
than deeply affecting; but in grace and melody they have
seldom been surpassed. Those that relate to the wrongs of
Ireland, and the fate of her patriots are particularly beautiful. There is more real feeling in them than in any of
his other verses. For Moore was a thorough Irishman.
He had all the wit, the versatility, the fickleness and the
vanity of that gifted, but unfortunate race, and he has embodied the spirit of his nation in these beautiful songs.

On turning to his prose works the first that attracts our
attention is the „Epicurean“. It is a romance, the plot of
which is laid in Egypt, during the first ages of Christianity.
The hero is a young philosopher, who has come to Egypt
to learn wisdom from the mouths of the priests and sages of
that land of marvels. Dissatisfied with their teachings and
the long and tedious years of trial through which he has to
pass, he meets a Christian who converts him. The characters are not well drawn, nor is the change in the heroes opinions well conceived or carefully enough executed, but some
of the scenes are very striking. It is not however a very
powerful tale nor is it now generally read.

The only works of Moore which still remain to be noticed are his biographies. The best of these is the life of
Lord Byron, one of the best works of the kind in our language. It is carefully arranged and well written, and is deservedly a great favourite with all who are interested in the
literary history of that age.

His works as a whole are rather light and graceful essays than masterpieces of art. He was gifted with fancy
rather than imagination. He could not paint either characters or passion with much force, but he could write cleverly
and even poetically about them. All the minor talents of
a poet he possessed in a high degree. In melody of rhythm,
ease of style, and variety of imagery he has seldom been surpassed. His colouring is always gorgeous, and his narrative
poems are sometimes overladen with ornament. His lyrical
poetry on the other hand is always graceful, and generally
simple. His songs are to be found in every Irish house, and
they are sung at every Irish festival. This was probably what
induced Byron to call him the Irish Burns. This title has
been so often repeated that it has now become proverbial,
yet no nickname could be more inappropriate. Both poets
were, it is true, the authors of popular songs; but there the
resemblance ceases. Burns was a realist in art. He drew
men and things as he saw them. Like a Dutch painter he
chose his subjects from every-day life. He loved to paint
the village ale-house, the peasant's fireside, and the popular
festivals of Scotland. Moore loved to revel in imaginary scenes.
He placed his heroes in distant countries, and among circumstances as unlike his own as possible. His pictures have always something dreamy about them. He delights in the daz-
zling splendour of the East, in halls hung with gorgeous
drapery, and glittering with costly jewels. The air of the enchanted land he loves to paint is faint with the perfume of roses.
The light that he throws upon his characters is tinted with
rainbow hues. Again, Burns excels in characteristic. His
peasants are men such as you meet in the fields. Their
hands are hardened by work. They are not, it is true, elegant and heroic, but they are men. His women characters
are rosy-cheeked peasant girls, not high born ladies, but what
is wanting in elegance is made up for in truth. Moore, on
the other hand, is so anxious to make his characters heroic

and graceful that he forgets to make them men and women.
One feels that they can only exist in the fairy land which he
has created for them.   Finally Burns's songs are forcible and
immediate bursts of emotion.   In reading them, we feel that
they are true — as true as nature itself.   Moore, at best,
only describes passion, and the finest of his songs are those
which are purely reflective.

We have now come to the end of our first group of poets.
We have seen that, in spite of the originallity of each, they
had much in common. They were all narrative poets, and all of
them laid the scenes of their narratives in distant lands and times.
They loved to describe the heroic and the unusual, or at least
the distant. Some of Scott's novels seem, it is true, to be exceptions, but none of them can be called tales of every-day life.

CHAPTER V.

Our second group consists of the poets who formed
what was then called the „Lake school“.   Wordsworth and
Coleridge are the chief of these.   The tie that united them
was rather external than internal. Their poetical opinions and
theories differed widely. So did the character of their works.
But they were friends, they understood and loved each other.
They constantly defended each other when attacked by the
critics.   Hence they began to be looked upon as a school of
poets, who strove for the same end, and submitted to the
same critical laws. This belief was so general, and it has left
so deep an impress on our critical literature, that it would be
very difficult to separate them; and the inconvenience would
far out-weigh any advantages which might result from a
more scrupulous correctness.

William Wordsworth was by far the greatest poet of
the Lake school. Indeed he is considered by many the great-

est poet of tho period. The influence of his poetry was not
so quickly and widely felt as that of Byron, but it was deeper and more permanent. For years he laboured on, amid
the scorn of his contemporaries, certain that the works he
wrote would be unpopular, but certain also that they would
be immortal. He was not generally acknowledged to be a
poet till he was an old man, but his writings contain no complaints of this injustice. It would have been impossible for
Byron or Scott to have done this. They hungered after present fame and present profit. Wordsworth, though not
careless of fame, wrote mainly from a pure love of writing.
He moulded and polished and finished off his verses with a
care which is a striking contrast to the haste with which his
more brilliant contemporaries dashed off their works. His
life had little in it that was either striking or interesting,
but it was the life of all others best suited to a philosophical
poet. He lived by the lakes he loved so well, with his wife
and sister, satisfied with the simple pleasures of country life.
He spent his time in his garden, amid his books, and in wandering alone or with his sister through the beautiful scenery which surrounded his house, meditating or conversing
with the simple hearted peasantry who surrounded him.
Yet it is pleasant to turn from the splendour of Abbotsford,
and from the scenes of glittering dissipation amid which Byron moved, to Wordsworth's humble cottage at Grasmere
or Rydal mount. It is pleasant to hear of the primative
hospitality to be found there, and of the kindly care with
which the poet strove to diminish the hardships, and increase the pleasures of his poorer neighbours. Scott too
took an interest in the affairs of his tenantry, and he was
always ready with a kind word and a helping hand, to
assist them in trouble. But this was one of his many luxu-
ries, while it was one of the principal ends of Wordsworth's
life. But it is not with the man but the poet that we have
to do. More than any of his English contemporaries he

7 *

wrote with a purpose.   Most of our great poets, during this
age, gave free scope to their imagination, and let it carry
them where it would.   They did not inquire into the principles of art, or, if they did, their studies had but little effect on their poems.   Wordsworth, on the other hand, had
a theory of poetry, and this theory had a great effect on his
verses.   It certainly did not make him a poet; indeed, it
seems to me, to have often rather injured his poetry than
otherwise; but it certainly directed his poetical talents.   It
is only justice to confess, that his one-sided theory did not
make him one-sided in his judgement of others.   He had not,
it is true, a catholic taste; but his dislike of Wilhelm Meister
and the poetry of Byron arose from moral, and not from aesthetical scruples.   He liked the works of Scott, and was passionately fond of our early poets, who differed from him as
widely as possible.

While the group of poets whose works we have examined were seeking their subjects in distant lands and ages, he
directed his attention to every day modern life.   Here, he
contended, was the true material for modern poetry.   The age
of chivalry was beautiful, and it doubtless contained subjects
of high poetical interest, but it is past.   Its poets did well
to sing about it, for they were its exponents.   But modern
life has also its beauties, its noble struggles, and its poetical
motives, if we had only eyes to see them, and it is with these
that we have to do.   God, man, and nature are still the same,
and it is the duty of the poet of the nineteenth century to
show, that his own age too is God-like, noble, and beautiful.
He must free its beauty and truth from the dust that veils it
from common eyes.   It avails us little to know, how a man
might live a pure and noble life in centuries and forms of society long since past away, we must show how it is possible
for him to do it to-day.   He is never weary of repeating
that the common-place affairs of every day life only appear

unpoetical to us because our own eyes are not capable of dis-
covering their beauty. Thus in one of his poems he writes

Long have I loved what I behold,
The night that calms, the day that cheers;
The common growth of mother earth
Suffices me — her tears and mirth,
Her humblest mirth and tears.

The dragon's wing, the magic ring,
I shall not covet for my dower,
If I along that lowly way
With sympathetic heart may stray,
And with a soul of power.

It is not strange that, having gone thus far, he should
go farther, that after insisting on truth to nature, and on
making common feelings the subjects of poetry, he should
insist on their being expressed in common words. Hence
his celebrated theory of poetical language, which caused the
witty remark of Byron

He both by precept and example shows
That prose is verse, and verse is merely prose.

But this remark is as unjust as satire usually is. Wordsworth merely meant, that the language should be suited to
the subject, and that the taste for high flown phrases, which
was so common in his age, was false. That he was right
in this no one in our days will deny.

We will now cast a hasty glance at a few of his works.
The first of these, which has any great importance, was entitled „Lyrical ballads". This work was greeted by a storm
of hostile criticism, which the most partial critic cannot say
was entirely undeserved. His theories here were carried to
an extreme which bordered on caricature. The subjects can
hardly be said to be c h o s e n from common life, they were
mere transcrpts of whatever came first. Sometimes it is impossible to tell whether the poet intends to be serious or hu-

mourous.   The language and rhythm, of many pieces were
mannerised in the highest degree.   Now a mere copy of
every-day life is worth nothing.   The greatest English poets
who, before the time of Wordsworth, had painted it realistically were Chaucer and Burns.   But they had either treated
their subjects humourously, or rendered them poetical by
colouring them with deep passion.   Wordsworth did neither.
Yet some of the poems have a simple grace and delicacy that
it would be difficult to match elsewhere.

But rustic and idyllic subjects do not make up the whole
of modern life, or even the most poetical part of it.   This
Wordsworth felt, and, in his long meditative walks, his mind
was often busied with subjects very different from those he
treated in the lyrical ballads.   While his eyes were always
open to catch the most fitful shades of natural beauty, he
was pondering deeply over the great questions of life, and
death, and immortality.   These were the subjects which he
now resolved to treat poetically.   Hence the „Excursion" was
produced.   This is his great masterpiece.   It is a philosophical
but not a didactic poem.   Wordsworth was far too great a
poet to wander back to the dreary regions in which the poets
of the classical school had loved to linger.   He saw that the
creation of beauty, and not the discovery of truth, was the
great end of poetry.   He believed with Hegel that beauty
has a right to exist for its own sake alone, or as he phrased
it, that „the end of poetry is to produce excitement in coexis-
tence with an overbalance of pleasure".   He knew well enough
that no good end could be answered by writing philosophical
treatises in rhyme.   But there are arguments drawn from experience, might not they be stated in verse that should deserve the name of poetry?   Let us take an example.   Few
indeed of the many thousands who have read with delight
the simple poem „We are seven" ever imagined that it was
intended by its author to be a serious argument for the immortality of the soul.Yet such was the fact.   No child or un-

sophisticated person, argued the poet, ever imagines the possibility of anihilation. They feel instinctively that their lives must endure forever. This is not the result of religious training; it is the natural feeling which is common to all mankind. Now let us examine his poetical statement of it.

We are Seven.

A simple child,
That lightly draws its breath,
And feels its life in every limb,
What should it know of death?

I met a little cottage girl:
She was eight years old, she said;
Her hair was thick with many a curl
That clustered round her head.

She had a rustic woodland air,
And she was wildly clad:
Her eyes were fair and very fair; —
Her beauty made me glad.

„Sisters and brothers, little Maid,
How many may you be?“
„How many? Seven in all“, she said,
And wondering looked at me.

„And where are they? I pray you tell“
She answered „Seven are we;
And two of us at Conway dwell, ,
And two are gone to sea.

Two of us in the church-yard lie,
My sister and my brother,
And in the church-yard cottage I
Dwell near them with my mother!“

„You say that two at Conway dwell,
And two are gone to sea,

Yet ye are seven! — I pray you tell,
Sweet Maid, how this may be".

Then did the little Maid reply,
„Seven boys and girls are we:
Two of us in the church-yard lie,
Beneath the church-yard tree!"

„You run about, my little Maid,
Your limbs they are alive;
If two are in the church-yard laid,
Then ye are only five."

„Their graves are green, they may be seen",
The little Maid replied,
„Twelve steps, or more, from mother's door,
And they are side by side.

My stockings there I often knit,
My kerchief there I hem;
And there upon the ground I sit,
And sing a song to them.

And often after sunset, Sir,
When it is light and fair,
I take my little porringer,
And eat my supper there.

The first that died was sister Jane,
In bed she moaning lay,
Till God released her from her pain;
And then she went away.

So in the church-yard she was laid;
And when the grass was dry,
Together round her grave we played,
My brother John, and I.

And when the ground was white with snow,
And I could run and slide,

My brother John was forced to go,
And he lies by her side!"

„How many are you then", said I,
„If they two are in heaven?"
Quick was the little Maid's reply,
„O, Master! we are seven."

„But they are dead; those two are dead!
Their spirits are in heaven!"
I was throwing words away; for still
The little Maid would have her will,
„Nay, Master! we are seven."

Here there is no dull statement of the argument, no
subtle reasoning; he describes a simple natural scene, and
leaves his readers to deduce the argument from it, as they
might have done from the fact itself. The value of the argument as an argument does not, of course, concern us here.
We have only to do with Wordsworth's way of stating it poetically. But this is not the only way of writing a philosophical
poem; it is not the way in which his greatest philosophical
poems are written. Modern life was in his opinion the proper subject for poetry, it was the material out of which poems
should be formed, but the mood of mind in which the subject was to be approached, the forms into which this raw
material was to be cast were still left to the option of the
poet. He was not obliged to put aside the rich hoard of re-
flection with which his mind was stored when he began to
speak of common things. Might he not, after having formed
a theory of the world by means of long experience, and deep
meditation, arrange his facts and observations, his tales of
human life, and his descriptions of natural scenery, in such
a way as to illustrate his theory. Such a plan had many obvious advantages. The simplest tale would cease to be common place, because it would be brought into connexion with
the great idea of the universe For every day life is unin-

teresting, not because it is common, but because it seems to
be accidental, a thing quite apart from our noblest thoughts,
and our highest aspirations. How if it could be brought into
harmony with them? Would not it then gain a quite new
significance? This is the idea of the „Excursion". The plan
of the poem is simply and unskillfully constructed. It is
merely the account of a three days walk among the hills, of
the scenes he passed through, and the people he met. He
intended it to form a part of a much greater work, „The Recluse", which was to treat „the sensations and opinions of a poet
living in retirement". This work was never completed. The
Excursion is masterly in the highest degree. Never, since
the days of Milton, had blank verse so sonorous and so
nervous been written in England. The descriptions of scenery, though they have not the fire and spirited dash of Byron about them, betray a much nearer acquaintance with
nature, and a much deeper sympathy with it, than those of
his more brilliant rival. The spirit too that breathes through
the whole poem is that of the deepest reverence — of reverence for man, reverence for nature, and for nature's God.

Some of the pictures of human life in this poem are very
striking and powerful. Among these that of the Solitary
takes a high place. He was the son of humble parents and
educated for the ministry, but his heart was too bold, and
his spirits too high for him to relish the quiet life of a country clergyman. He therefore became the chaplain of a
troup of soldiers, and lived among them,

> Lax, boyant; less a pastor with his flock
> Than a soldier among soldiers.

At last he met, and fell in love with a lady of beauty,
taste, and fortune. With her he retired to his old home, and
they lived very happily, till

> — Death suddenly o'erthrew
> Two lovely children, all that they possessed,
> The mother followed; miserably bare

The one survivor stood. We wept, he prayed
For his dismissal, day and night, compelled
By pain to turn his thoughts toward the grave,
And face the regions of eternity.
From this passionate grief he passed into apathy. The
news of the French revolution awoke him from his lethargy,
and he travelled to Paris, inspired by the wild hope which
then filled Europe. There for a time he lived preaching
    The cause of Christ and civil liberty
    As one, and moving to one glorious end.
Here his belief, which up to this time had been sincere,
was undermined, and, though he continued to preach, he
ceased to believe the religion in which he had been educated. At last the great day of disenchantment came, and he
saw that the freedom which he had worshipped was a dream.
He left France, and settled again in England. Here the poet
meets him, sunk in the lowest despair, scorning mankind
and himself.

We have not time to linger over the „White doe of
Rylstone“, or his other long poems. Many of his lyrics
are exquisite. Those addressed to Lucy, who seems to have
been his first love, are full of deep feeling, and all of them
have a simplicity which is strangely attractive. The lines to
his wife are perhaps the best known of all his poems. They
were written long after his marriage and are very characteristic.

                    A portrait.
She was a phantom of delight, ·
When first she gleamed upon my sight;
A lovly apparition, sent
To be a moment's ornament;
Her eyes as stars of twilight fair;
Like twilight's, too, her dusky hair;
But all things else about her drawn
From May-time a the cheerful dawn;

A dancing shape, an image gay,
To haunt, to startle, and waylay.

I saw her upon nearer view,
A spirit, yet a woman too!
Her household motions light and free,
And steps of virgin liberty;
A countenance in which did meet
Sweet records, promises as sweet;
A creature not too bright and good
For human nature's daily food;
For transient sorrows, simple wiles,
Praise, blame, love, kisses, tears and smiles.

And now I see with eye serene
The very pulse of the machine;
A being breathing thoughtful breath,
A traveller betwixt life and death;
The reason firm, the temperate will,
Endurance, forsight, strength and skill,
A perfect woman, nobly planned,
To warn, to comfort and command;
And yet a spirit still, and bright
With something of an angel light.

It was not, as we have already seen, in expressing deep
passion that Wordsworth excelled, but in quiet musings, and
descriptions of scenery. No form of verse is better suited
for such poetry than the sonnet. Accordingly we find that
he has left behind him a vast number of poems of this kind;
and in sonnet writing he reigns supreme. Almost all our
great poets have tried their hands at this form of verse,
but Milton alone can be compared to Wordsworth, and he
has left us not more than twenty sonnets, while Wordsworth's may be counted by hundreds. They are all finished

off with great care. With respect to the form of verse itself he says

> Nuns fret not at their convents narrow room,
> And hermits are contented with their cells,
> And students with their pensive citadels,
> Maids at the wheel, the weaver at his loom
> Sit blithe and happy; bees, that soar for bloom
> High as the highest peak of Furness Fells,
> Will murmur by the hour in fox-glove bells.
> In truth, the prison unto which we doom
> Ourselves no prison is, and hence to me,
> In sundry moods, twas pastime to be bound
> Within the sonnets scanty plot of ground;
> Pleased if some souls, for such there needs must be,
> Who have felt the weight of too much liberty,
> Should find short solace there, as I have found.

His patriotic sonnets deserve mention as he is the only
really great English poet of this age who took England's side
against Napoleon in verse that can be called poetry. The
verses themselves have great beauties, some of them indeed
are almost perfect.

In Wordsworth's works we find neither the lively characteristic of Scott, nor the deep titanic passion of Byron.
Still less do we find any trace of the light wit, and sprightly
fancy of Moore. He dealt with other subjects, and sought
other beauties — beauties which, if they are less striking,
are at least as enduring as those of his more popular contemporaries. It is a remarkable fact that, while Byron is falling into the shade and even Scott is less read than formerly,
the fame and influence of Wordsworth are steadily increasing. He has educated the public taste to an appreciation of
his works. In his youth he was ridiculed, in his old age he
was admired, now he is reverenced. This is easily accoun-
ted for. The faults of his poetry all lie on the surface, and
are visible to the most careless reader, while its beauties ap-

peal only to the reflective and observant. His verse is often
harsh, and his diction is seldom happily chosen. His style,
and the nature of his subjects were new; and they were not
brilliant. The most casual reader feels that the plan of several even of his noblest works is clumsy, and inartistic, and
that the subjects of many of his smaller poems are trivial;
but not one in a thousand, even of his admirers, perceives
the wonderful truth of his descriptions of nature. No English poet, with the exception of Shakspeare, can be compared with him in this respect. No tone is too soft to catch
his ear, no shadowing too slight to attract his eye. The
truth of his details is marvellous. He notes all the apparently
unimportant facts which, for the most part, are known only
to the landscape painter, and reproduces them with a truth
that the greatest landscape painter might envy. This is not
so slight or easy a thing as it at first seems. It is not till we
endeavour to observe nature carefully that we discover the difficulty of doing so. A landscape, or an effect of light and
shade impresses us as a whole, but very few attempt to analyze the feeling, and still fewer can point out the various
causes that produced it, or divide the necessary from the
accidental parts of a scene. Hence comes the difficulty that
young painters feel in copying correctly the colours of a giv-
en piece of scenery. One of the greatest of English artists
is said to have told a young painter that to look at nature
was the most difficult part of art. How little we do look at
nature, in the sense in which he used the words, we feel
when we endeavour to form an opinion of a painting. How
seldom are we able to say with certainty, this or that part
of the picture is true or false. When we reflect on this, we
shall not wonder that the first critics of Wordsworth did not
perceive the fineness of his detail. In fact one must take the
Excursion into the fields and woods, and compare it line by
line with nature, before we can appreciate its wonderful
exactness. Yet in his later works the poet seldom or ever

fell into the common fault of describing for the mere sake of describing; he used his wonderful knowledge either as illustration, or in painting a back ground for his human characters.

When we turn to these characters, it is true, we find that the poet is less happy in his mode of painting them. He had not the talent of depicting the external appearance of men and women which Scott possessed in so extraordinary a degree. We often find, it is true, realistic touches of wonderful truth, but it is too often generalized and not individualized truth. He seems to have observed children, for example, in nearly the same way in which he observed the cows and sheep browsing on the hills. He noticed what children as a rule would say and do, not what a particular child would say and do under given circumstances. Hence he describes childhood rather than children. He gives us what is common to all, not what is peculiar to each. Closely connected with this is another of his faults. In describing persons and events he does not sufficiently distinguish between the necessary and the accidental. This is the stranger because his descriptions of scenery are remarkably free from this fault, it is however the case, in many of his earlier poems. A great artist omits all that is unimportant. He reproduces with care every trait that can help to produce the effect he intends, and leaves out the rest. He knows that all that does not help hinders. Sometimes, it is true, it is at first difficult for the reader to say why this or that little circumstance was inserted, but a deeper consideration will show a reason for each. If we take Alexis and Dora for example, the most perfect of all modern idyls, we shall find this to be the case. As Alexis leaves his fathers house, after receiving his blessing, his mother places in his hand a bundle that she has made up after his other things had been sent away, and bearing it under his arm he leaves them. This little touch gives a perfect air of reality to the tale, but as soon as this end has been answered the bundle would only be in the way,

and we lose sight of it. Wordsworth would have followed
it as closely as Alexis. He would have told us how he put
it down, when he entered Dora's garden, and took it up
when he left it. It is needless to say that this would have
greatly weakened the effect. This is the case with many of
his scenes and characters. He tells us a thousand circumstances that do not help on the story, a thousand traits that
are not characteristic. But if in this respect he is inferior
to Scott, we must confess that he is in some respects superior,
to that great story-teller, even when dealing with human
nature. Neither Scott nor Byron could have equaled the conception of the Solitary, neither of them could have described
the internal life of a character so different from their own.
That is Wordsworth's great power. He sees the connection of
thought, feeling and action. He can conceive a spiritual
disease, he can point out its cause, trace its symptoms, and
tell its cure. The way in which he describes the Solitary's
case is masterly. It betrays a knowledge of human nature,
and the principles of human action, that Scott with all his
powers did not possess. Had the talents of these three poets
been united in one we should have had a second Shakespeare.

Another want in Wordsworth's nature was sensuousness,
a quality which all artistic geniuses of the highest order possess. It is this want which will prevent him ever being a
popular poet. Spite his own principles of criticism he does
not love beauty for its own sake, he saturates it with thought;
and his love for it decreases in exact proportion to its sensuousness. In his poetical affection inanimate nature came
first; then the inferior animals, and then children. The few
love poems he has written are singularly aërial and unreal. He
shrinks from describing the beauty of his love directly, as
surely poet never did before. He chooses his images, not
to make her beauty apparent, but to veil it. He compares
Lucy to a violet half hidden by a mossy stone, and to a star;
his wife is a phantom of delight, and a spirit. He delighted

in nature, it is true, he loved its beauty as few men have
loved it. Yet it was to him a symbol, and, beautiful as he
felt it to be, he loved the hidden meaning more than the
outward sign. Hence his reverence for the lakes and mountains, and the feeling of awe with which he moved among
them. This brings us to the secret of the truth of his description of scenery, and to their great difference from those
of Lord Byron. The latter poet looked at nature as a store-
house, from which he could take and leave what suited his
fancy. He too used it as a symbol for his woe, but while
he did so he felt that the use was arbitrary. Wordsworth, on
the other hand, felt that in dealing with it he was dealing
with a holy thing. He tried to woo it to tell its secrets, to
explain its hidden significance. It was his friend, his love,
his teacher, and his comforter. „To me", he says in the
noblest of his poems

„To me the humblest flower that blows can give
Thoughts that do often lie to deep for tears".

The finest of Wordsworth's poems are those in which
this feeling has free room, and among these the noblest seems
to me to be his „Ode on Intimations of Immortality from
Recollections of early Childhood". Emerson has called it the
high water-mark of English poetry, and it would certainly
be difficult to find, in the whole range of our literature, a
poem of the same class which is worthy to be placed beside it.

Samuel Taylor Coleridge was one of the most remarkable
men England ever produced. In talents he was equal to any
poet of his age, in learning he was superior to them all; yet
he produced no great masterpiece. His works are a series of
fragments. They have a marvellous beauty, it is true, and
are without exception the most original productions of the
age, but they are still only the signs of what he might have
done. Sometimes a few words of his hint at long trains of
thought or summon up forms of wonderful beauty, but before the mind can grasp them they have vanished. He is the

most suggestive of English poets, but then his works only
suggest. Hence, though his influence on our literature has
been great, it has been indirect. He was the first to introduce
the modern metrical romance, but it was Scott and Byron
who reaped the harvest of fame and wealth from this style of
writing. He was the first Englishman who studied and to a
certain degree appropriated the ideas of German philosophy,
but the praise was lavished on his disciples. Finally, it was
he who first introduced into England the principles of philosophic criticism, but his scholars, who cannot be compared
with him either in learning or taste, have forced their way into the place that he should have occupied. This was doubtless owing to the want of mental concentration, which seems
to have been an organic defect of his mind, but which was
increased by his excessive use of opium as a stimulant. Besides this he had that inveterate habit of day-dreaming
which is often mistaken for indolence, but which is in fact a
state of great mental activity. He loved it to lose himself in
dreams of future works. He delighted in what Balzac calls intellectual cegar smoking. He was perpetually forming plans.
This is at once the highest pleasure, and the greatest danger
of an artist. So much seems to be done when a great thought
has been grasped, or a great plan conceived, and the mechanical labour of composition seems at once so unimportant and so dry, that a man of great imagination, or subtle
intellect seldom or ever overcomes the habit when he has
once sunk into it. This was the case with Coleridge. His
conversation was filled with brilliant thoughts and pictures.
The most intellectual and refined society in London thronged
his rooms to hear him explain philosophical systems, which,
had he written them, would, as they unanimously assure us,
have gained him a place among the greatest of modern philosophers, but he never wrote down more than a few scat-
tered thoughts, so that we are obliged to guess at his inte-

lectual power by a few written fragments, and the imperfect reports of his conversations which remain.

The most important of Coleridge's poems is „Christabel." It is the fragment of a metrical romance, and was the first of its kind. From it Scott learned the form of Marmion and the lady of the Lake, but the spirit of Coleridge's poem is very different from that of Scott's. It approaches much nearer to that of the old romances. It is a wierd tale of enchantments and wonders. The dim light through which the characters move reminds one strongly of the novels of Fouqué; but it is much more powerfully written than the Zauber-ring. The rhythm of this poem is strikingly melodious. It differs from the melody of Moore's best verses just as the music of the wind amid the pine boughs, or the sound of an Aeolean harp differs from a song of Verdi's. Sometimes it reminds one of long forgotten melodies, sometimes it suggests music far wilder and sweeter than its own. Short passages fix themselves in the memory, not on account of their sense so much as their music. We repeat them to ourselves just as we hum over an old tune without thinking of the meaning. The imagery of the poem is exceedingly beautiful. The poet's vast and curious learning opened up to him stores of illustration that were hidden from his less learned contemporaries. He was deeply read in the poetical and mystical literature of the middle ages, and this gave a colouring to his verses. His very style spoke of his acquaintance with our old poets; and the fine taste with which he selected the form of expression which suited his subject cannot be too highly praised. The diction of Christabel is just antiquated enough to give it the rich flavour of age. It abounds in phrases and forms of expression that are now obsolete, but it is never so antiquated as to render it difficult for the most unlearned reader to understand it.

„The Ancient Mariner" has some points of resemblance with Christabel. It is, like it, a tale of supernatural won-

8 *

ders, but they are of a very different description. They have
a seriousness about them that has something aweful in it.
Above all, the dreaminess which gives such a charm to Christabel is wanting here, but in its place we have a clearness
which is far better suited to this subject.

Coleridge's dramas are better than those of Byron and
Scott. They have great poetical beauties though but little
dramatic power. His translation of Wallenstein occupies a
very high, if not the highest place, among our metrical translations. His smaller poems are, taken as a whole, hardly
equal to their fame.

The mind of Coleridge was endowed with vast, and very
dissimilar powers. He was at once a poet and a man of deep
learning. In both of these characters too he displayed an
uncommonly large range of powers. Some of his poems have
much of the dreamy beauty and melody of Shelley, while, in
his dramas, the firmness of his touch often reminds us of
Scott. On the other hand he was equally acquainted with
the dreamy systems of the mystics, and the clear logic of the
modern German philosophers. In his later years, most of
his time was taken up in planning two great works, neither
of which was executed. The one was a treatise on the
„Word“ in the Gospel according to St. John; the other was a
new system of philosophy, founded on that of Kant. Probably no single Englishman of the age could have undertaken
either with so much hope of success. When we remember
that his remarks on Shakespeare are beyond all comparison
the finest essays on that poet in our language, we shall at
once see that his was a mind of no ordinary power. But this
power was to a great extent lost, from his incurable want of
method and power of will. The sad lines which he addressed to Wordsworth are but to true.

Ah! as I listened with a heart forlorn,
The pulses of my being beat anew;
And even as life returns unto the drowned,

Life's joy rekindling roused a throng of pains —
Keen pangs of Love, awakening as a babe
Turbulent, with an outcry in the heart;
, And fears self-willed, that shunned the eye of hope;
And hope that scarce would know itself from fear;
Sense of past youth, and manhood come in vain,
And genius given, and knowledge won in vain;
And all which I had culled in wood-walks wild,
And all which patient toil had reared, and all
Commune with thee had opened out — but flowers
Strewed on my corse, and borne upon my bier,
In the same coffin, for the self-same grave!

It is impossible to criticise the verses which he has left
us as a whole, impossible to say where his power began and
where it ended, for they are all only fragments. WHe read
them with delight, but we are not satisfied; they are all only
hints of what might have been, and is not. He has been
charged with obscurity, but his obscurity is never verbal.
His trains of thought are to deep to be expressed with all
the clearness of Byron or Scott, and he merely hints at, and
seldom expresses his thought. His imagery, too, is certainly
less sharp than that of the two poets I have just mentioned,
but this arises from no want of distinctness in the pictures
themselves, nor from any fault of the language in which
they are clothed. It is, so to speak, part of his technic.
He shadows his poetic forms in a mist; but it is no ordinary
dreary fog that envelops them, but a golden haze, like that
caused by the sunlight falling on rain.- The very indistinctness adds to the charm. In that peculiar kind of imagination which gives birth to mythologies and forms of religion,
Shelley is the only poet of the age who can be compared to
him. This faculty is one which is seldom to be found in
civilized society. It is one of the powers of which education
seems to rob us, we have lost is as we have lost the keenness
of our senses. Among the poets of the middle ages it was de-

veloped to an extraordinary degree, as the story of Arthur,
the Holy Grail and a thousand other myths show. But in no
English writer of the middle ages do we find it more clearly
exhibited, than in the writings of Coleridge and Shelley.
We cannot better conclude this short sketch of his poetry
than by an extract from Ferd. Freiligrath's biographical me-
moir of the poet.

„Coleridge, with all his errors and shortcomings, is
yet a name never to be omitted in a history of the march of
the English mind. Not so much for what he has actually
performed, as for the stimulating impulses given by him.
His gifts were of the richest and highest order, yet, however powerful as a critic, however profound as a metaphysician, however melodious and imaginative as a poet, he from
an innate want of courage and energy of character had it
not in his power to give to his faculties that development,
which, if it had been attained, would entitle him to one of
the very highest places in English literature“.

The critic then traces Coleridge's influence in promoting
„that all important exchange of ideas between two great kindred nations, which at present, stirring and humanising,
fluctuates to and fro across the German Ocean“. He then
proceeds, „For a metaphysician, Coleridge was perhaps too
imaginative; for a poet, may be, too metaphysical. At least
some of his earlier poems (not the very earliest * * *) are
of a greater abstruseness, than would seem pardonable in a
poet. His later and maturer effusions happily avoid this defect. They are, even if their subject-matter is wild and
fanciful, simple and natural in expression, and full of a music
which, in the English language, has rarely been surpassed.
.... Altogether, there was little of the plastic artist in Coleridge. He is sometimes a painter, but never a sculptor.
Life, palpable reality are things which evade his grasp. His
domain lies in Cloudland; his world is but too often a visio-

nary world. Hence, let us not forget, the insufficiency of his dramatic attempts; hence, too, the otherwise startling and inexplicable fact, that his voyage to the South has been utterly resultless to his poetry."

The works of Coleridge may be looked upon as the connecting link between our second and third group. To this we must now pass; for, though the works of Southey are by no means unimportant, he cannot claim a place among the greatest writers of the age.

CHAPTER VI.

The story of *Percy Bysshe Shelley's* life is as strange as any romance could be, far stranger, nobler and perhaps even sadder than that of Byron, which set all the world weeping It is, however, but very imperfectly known. No really trustworthy biography has as yet appeared, and we are obliged to collect stray hints from the writings of his contemporaries, and to test by them the trustworthiness of the different sketches of his life or of parts of it which from time to time are published. His poetry has had the same fate as that of Wordsworth. At the time of its publication it was laughed at, or treated with entire indifference, but since his death its popularity has daily increased, until now it equals that of Byron, while his influence on óur literature has been nearly as great as that of Wordsworth. He was born on the 4th August 1792. His father was Sir Thomas Shelley, one of the richest baronets in Surrey. He seems to have been a rough man, strongly conservative in his political views, and fond of hunting; not at all capable of understanding the sensitive nature of his son. At ten years old the poet was sent to Sion house school, but his life there does not seem to have been a happy one. Nor were matters much 'im-

proved when he was removed to Eton. The system of fag-
ging which still exists there was then carried to an incredible extent. Shelley's fine sense of justice was outraged
at every turn. It was here, if we may believe his own account, that he made the great resolution of his life to stand
on the side of the weak against the strong, and of truth
against error.

His resolution was only too well kept, and from that hour
his life was a protest against injustice and falsehood. Such
were the feelings with which he went to Oxford, the seat of
conservatism and orthodoxy. He studied hard, but not the
subjects which are generally studied there. The works of
Plato and the Neoplatonists occupied much of his time; but
the German and Italian literature, and the philosophy of Germany and France, seem to have been the principal objects of
his study. The writings of the encyclopaedists led him to
the natural sciences; and he spent much of his time over
his microscope and in chemical experiments. We have several pictures of him at this time from his fellow students.
We hear much of his bright face, and the eagerness with
which he disputed on any subject, which lay near his heart,
and still more of his gentleness and charity. At this time
Shelley imbibed atheistic principles. He was probably predis-
posed to heterodoxy, for he had seen Christianity in its most
unfavourable light. He had not seen it standing between
the oppressed and their oppressors, soothing the sick and
lighting up the cottages of the poor, but united with the
king and the nobles to resist what seemed to him the progress of mankind. He had found in its professors not love
but intolerance, not belief but bigotry. Hence its dogmas
had but little hold upon him, and he became an easy convert
to the opinions taught with such clear but superficial logic
in the „System of nature“. For a young man so much in
earnest as Shelley to form on opinion and to act upon it is
the same thing. He immediately composed, with the assis-

tance of a fellow-student, a pamphlet, entitled „The necessity of Atheism". It was in all probability a very weak
and daring work — a mere repetition of the arguments of
the French philosophers, of the age. In order to prevent
the possibility of its being passed over in silence, the authors
sent a copy of it to each of the professors, with a request
that they would answer it. The consequence was, that both
the authors were expelled from the university. This has often been blamed as an act of intolerance, but I cannot say
that it seems to me to have been unnecessarily harsh. We
may indeed regret that there was no man of riper years and
experience to take the young poet by the hand; but we must
not allow our sympathy for him to make us unjust to others.
Oxford was, at that time, a University founded on the principles of the Anglican church. Even protestant dissenters
were not permitted to study there. Hence she could not allow
books which were professedly heterodox to be published by
her students. The imprudent behaviour of the young men,
in sending the book to the professors, had rendered it impossible that its publication should be passed over in silence,
and it was obviously impossible that the academical teachers
of Oxford should enter into a discussion of such questions with
their own pupils. Still the effect of the expulsion on Shelley's life and opinions was very unfortunate. It confirmed
him in his Atheism, and it separated him farther than ever
from his family. Indeed it is said, that his father forbade his
mother and sisters to hold any communication with him, Before this time he had been deeply attached to his cousin Har-
riett Grove, now he was forbidden to have any intercourse
with her.

Shelley removed to London and there continued his studies, which now led him into still wilder theories. He saw
clearly that all the miseries to which human nature is subject
could not be traced back either to a false religion, or a tyran-
ical government; they must therefore, he argued, be attri-.

buted to the abnormal state of society; for the idea that evil
was necessary never entered his mind. The two great causes
of human wretchedness now seemed to him to be the institution
of marriage, and the unequal division of wealth. There can
be no doubt that he sincerely and disinterestedly believed in
this theory. Nor was his philanthropy confined to his opinions. He spent a great part of his time and money in relieving
the poor. Once indeed he pawned the great joy of his life,
his solar microscope, in order that he might at once relieve
the wants of a poor family. His own way of life was simple
in the extreme. He seldom drank anything but water, and
often lived for days on bread and raisins, which he bought
and eat while walking through the streets. For a long time
he hesitated whether he should devote himself to poetry or
metaphysics. In this state of mind he wrote „Queen Mab,“ an
unfortunate attempt to unite both. This poem was written
before Shelley had completed his eighteenth year. He did
not intend it for publication, but, a copy getting into the
hands of a bookseller, it was published withouth his knowledge and against his will. It is a mere collection of abstract theories, entirely unfit for poetical treatment; but,
wild and dreamy as they are, he believed in them so sincerely that to him they were passionate emotions rather than
cold trains of reasoning. Hence come the bright flashes of
poetry which are to be found here and there even in this
poem. The diction too already shows much of the nervous
force, clearness, and wild melody which distinguished his later works. The description of the Fairy queen, with which
the poem opens, is a wonderful flight of imagination for a
boy in his eighteenth year. The theories which form the
subject matter of Queen Mab are of course crude and wild in
the extreme, and it would be difficult to match the impiety of
some passages; but even here we find that Shelley's heart
was pure and true and loving. It was because he loved mankind with such a deep, passionate love that he hated the creeds

and governments which seemed to him to be their curse so
bitterly.

One of Shelley's sisters was at school in London, and
he frequently visited her. One day, as they were walking
in the garden together, they met one of her school fellows,
Harriet Westbrook, a pretty blonde of sixteen. She attracted
his attention, and finding her name was Harriet — the name
of his first love, he insisted on being introduced to her. He
made a deep impression on her, and the acquaintance soon
ripened into intimacy. This young lady he afterwards married, without the knowledge or consent of her parents or his
own, in August 1811. This exasperated his father, and well
it might. Miss Westbrook's father kept a coffee-house in
London, and the proud old Baronet could scarcely be expected to take such a daughter-in-law into his family. He
stopped his sons allowance, but the relations of the young
couple allowed them a sum of money sufficient for their wants.
For a time things went well enough, and many strange stories are told of their childishness. So imprudent a marriage
could not be expected to end well. They were separated.
No trustworthy account of the particulars has been published.
This is the one dark spot in Shelley's life, the only thing the
most rigid moralist can blame. Left in the dark as we are
with respect to the causes which induced him to take the
step, we cannot blame him very severely. The consequences
of the separation however cast a dark cloud over his life.
Mrs Shelley commited suicide. About this time the poet's father agreed to allow his son £ 800 a year. This he did because the estate was entailed on him. Shortly afterwards
Shelley was, by means of an old and most iniquitous law,
deprived of the guardianship of his own children, because he
was a declared atheist. The charge was based on some passages in Queen Mab. On the 10th of December 1816 Shelley married his second wife, Mary Godwin, the daughter of
an author of some celebrity in those days, who agreed with

the poet in his religious and social theories.   This lady was
a very talented and well educated woman, and they lived
very happily together till the poet's death.

The only important work which he published between
his first and his second marriage is a poem entitléd „Alastor
or the spirit of Solitude".   It is a strange, unreal, and sad
story of a poets life.   Human interest it has none.   It tells
how a young man wanders, without any definite intention,
through the whole world.   He has neither friends, home, nor
country.   At last he falls in love with a dream, and wanders
on seeking it in vain,   It is the embodiment of that yearn-
ing after fellowship which we feel when young, and it is
now a favourite book of dreamy boys and girls.   At the time
of its publication it passed unnoticed.

In 1816 Shelley had travelled on the-Continent at the
recommendation of his physicians, who thought him in danger of sinking into consumtion.   At Geneva he met Lord
Byron for the first time.   On his return to England he settled at Marlow.   Here „the Revolt of Islam", the longest of
his poems, was written.   We need not trace even the outline
of this strange story. It tells how a youth and maiden attempt
to reform the world by overthrowing tyranny and religion,
how they for awhile succeed, but are at last overthrown and
executed, upon which the poem follows them to the abode
of the blest. It is needless to say that the tale is improbable,
no incident in it could well have happened.   The characters too are not only unreal, they are impossible.   Yet they
are clearly and sharply drawn, and they have a certain truth.
They are true to our purest and highest thoughts.   They are
not what we are, but they are, spite their many errors,
what, in our highest moments, we should wish to be.   Shelley has often been blamed for painting dark and horrible pictures.   If this were true of any of his writings it would be
true of this.   Nowhere else, except in his Prometheus,
has he attempted a subject which gave him such room for

the description of horrors, and in that poem, he draws a veil over the sufferings of the Titan. In the revolt of Islam this is not the case, he does not attempt to disguise the pain and suffering with which he has to do, but before we blame him for this, we must ask whether it would have been possible for him to do so. He tells the story of the greatest self-sacrifice, and the most heroic daring for the human race, but to understand and sympathize with such actions we must feel that they are necessary, or they appear mere foolery if not something worse. Shelley never gloats over such descriptions with that unhealthy love of ugliness which so many modern poets have shown. He uses them as the dark background of a picture of truth and love. This poem too is the clearest statement of his creed, which he has left us. Men, he saw, were wretched, cruel and intolerant. He himself had suffered, as few equally pure men have ever suffered, from these faults; but these, he thought, were only the necessary results of accidental circumstances. Man, he is never tired of repeating, is not by nature bad; he is pure and holy; but he is blind. Show him the good and he will love it, aye and die for it. Teach him the lesson of love and he will sit at thy feet. It is his blindness, his ignorance, and madness which make him evil, but we must love him all the more for these, as a mother loves her crippled child better than the strong one who has less need of her care. Even the very tyrant who spreads desolation around him must not be hated but pitied. Alas! is not he the most unhappy of us all? We may have to fight against him, but let it not be in hate, but in sorrow, for is not he too a brother? This may be a dreamy idealism, but there is something in it which speaks to the hearts of the noblest of our young men, and it has done much to make Shelley's poems a book which stands to them in the place of a friend. The execution of the poem is rather unequal. It contains passages which are among the finest he ever wrote, and others which remind us strongly of the in-

coherencies of Queen Mab. The form of verse — the stanza
of Spenser, was excellently suited to the subject, and he
has treated it in masterly a manner, but it left little scope
for the wonderful and irregular bursts of melody which are
one of the great charms of many of his other poems.

While residing at Marlow Shelley continued his old habit of caring for the poor. No country clergyman could have
devoted his time more exclusively to his congregation than
the young poet did his to his poorer neighbours. Wherever
sickness, poverty, or sorrow was, there might Shelley be found,
with a kind word and a helping hand. Neither bad weather,
nor sickness could keep him away from these self imposed du-
ties. It was this self-devotion which brought on a severe
attack of illness that forced him to leave England for Italy
on the 12th of March 1818. He never returned to his native
country.

In Rome he wrote his „Prometheus unbound." There is
probably no mythological subject which has so deep an interest
for modern times as the story of Prometheus. It is, like Faust,
a tragedy whose basis is as broad as human nature. The plan
of Shelley's poem is so utterly different from that of Aeschylus
that they can not be compared with each other. It has a much
nearer resemblance, in spirit, to Goethe's marvellous fragment on the same subject. At least it will be more profitable
for us to compare them. Of course the power, the classical
clearness, and the admirable characteristic of the German
poem are wanting in the English one. Of course their can
be no comparison between Goethe and Shelley; but the ra-
dical difference between the two poets makes the comparison only the more interesting. We find that both aimed at
the same thing, both endeavoured to cast a modern idea into
an antique form — to use a classical myth as the dress of a
new thought. Goethe's fragment is unfortunately less known
than it deserves to be. Had it been completed, it would
take its stand among the noblest of his works. Shelley's

drama is perhaps of all his works the one which shows
his various powers to the most advantage. All the talents
which are displayed in it are perhaps shown to more advantage in some of his other poems, but here they are
united while in the others they can only be found singly.
The essential difference between the characters of the two
poets is to be seen at the most hasty glance at the plans of
the two works. Goethe was by nature a heathen; Shelley,
spite his Atheism and his almost fanatical hatred of the dogmas
of Christianity, was a Christian. Hence the leading idea of
the German work is purely artistic, that of the English purely moral. The Prometheus of Goethe treats of the struggle
between the individual and the universal good. His hero
is a being of Titanic might, who demands space for the exer-
cise of his powers. He has, he thinks, as much right to
his own world as the gods to theirs. Thus he says

That which I have they cannot take from me,
And that which they have let them guard themselves.
Here mine and thine.

To the question „What then belongs to thee?" he answers
„The circle that my power of working fills,
Nought under nor above".

Shelley's Prometheus is a very different character. He
is moved by no desire of mere personal freedom, he suffers
for the human race. In Goethe's poem the gods only seem
evil to Prometheus, here they are evil. That is the great
idea of the poem, the contest of good and evil. Evil, in
the person of Jupiter, sits crowned in heaven, all power
and might are given into his hands. His rule would be
unbounded, but for the lonely sufferer who hangs nailed to
peaks of the Caucasus. If he can be overcome, the power
of the gods can never be shaken, the good will be utterly
vanquished. If he remains unshaken, the day of deliverance
may, nay it must, come. The feeling that moves him is
love not pride. Like Christ on the cross, he suffers not for

himself, but for the salvation of the whole world. It is evident that such a contest can be terminated by no truce.   In
Goethe's poem. such a conclusion was possible, nay as it
seems to me, necessary.   His hero might, and I .believe
would have been brought to see that the good of the individual is not opposed to the laws of the universal — nay that
he can only find real happiness in submitting to those laws.
This conclusion is foreshadowed in the words with which his
brother leaves him, after he has refused the offer of Jupiter,

„Thou stand'st alone,
And in thy self-will dost despise the blessing,
That the gods, and thou,
And thine, the universe, and heaven, and earth
United in a single whole would feel.

In Shelley's Drama this was impossible, Prometheus
and Jupiter — good and evil — can never come to terms. One
of them must be crushed.   Hence it was necessary that the
poem should conclude with the fall of Jupiter.   We cannot
follow out the comparison farther, because the time chosen
by the two poets was different.   The German fragment ends
before the hero has been fastened to the rock.   Shelley's
drama does not begin till he has already hung there three
thousand years.   It opens with a monologue by Prometheus,
who hangs, chained to the precipice, with Jone and Panthea
seated at his feet.   He demands to hear the curse which he
spoke, when he was first condemned to his long anguish.
After the spirits of Earth and air have refused to speak, from
fear of Jupiter, a shade from the regions of the dead repeats
it.   Prometheus then exclaims

It doth repent me.   Words are quick and vain.
Grief for awhile is blind, and so was mine,
I wish no living thing to suffer pain.

On this Mercury appears, and offers peace on condition
of submission.   This is at once refused.   All bodily tortures
have now in vain been tried, a greater yet remains behind.

The furies summon up before him pictures of all human wretchedness and meanness; they show him men living and dying for their kind in vain, truths taught and battles fought in vain, hearts broken, and lives self-sacrificed in vain. These tortures are designed to show that Prometheus is struggling for a worthless race. Though crushed by the sight, his answer sounds clear and high:

, This is defeat, fierce king, not victory.
The sights with which thou torturest girl my soul
.With new endurance, till the hour arrives
When they shall be no types of things which are.

, The way in which the poet makes us feel the whole effects of the terrible scenes without bringing their horrors directly before our eyes is masterly in the extreme. As soon as the Furies withdraw, Prometheus is comforted by a chorus of spirits, who tell him of the pure and noble deeds that are done by mankind. Four lines will serve as a specimen. A spirit sings. „I alit

On a great ship lightning split,
And speeded hither on the sigh
Of one who gave his enemy
His plank, and plunged aside to die.

` Thus the first act terminates. We need not follow the progress of the drama farther. Jupiter is hurled from his throne, and the poem concludes with a magnificent series of choruses from the spirits of the delivered world.

· Shelley's next work was „the Cenci", a tragedy in five acts. During his residence in Rome, he had spent much of his time in the picture galleries of that city. He had there seen Guido Reni's picture of Beatrice Cenci, and it had made a deep impression on his mind. He himself says, he could get no rest till he had written the sad story of that beautiful and unfortunate lady. Her history is too well known for it to be necessary, to retell it. It is one of those stories which at once attract the dramatist by their striking contrasts, and

overwhelming passion. Ford or Massenger would have delighted in such a subject, but most modern poets would have
shrunk from it with horror. Indeed there were almost insu-
perable difficulties in the way of its artistic treatment. Shelley
did not entirely overcome them. The Cenci is far from being
faultless in an aesthetical point of view, but it is incomparably
the best modern English drama. It shows that Shelley possessed powers which are displayed in none of his other works,
that he could draw human characters and natural passion
with as much power as the wild and aërial dreams in which
he chiefly delighted. The first scene of the tragedy awakens
our interest, and it never flags till the end of the last, when
Beatrice is led out to execution. Yet the drama has its
faults. The character of Count Cenci is, if not unnaturally, at
least inartistically evil. This fault lay in the nature of the
subject. The Count, as history and tradition represent him,
was as near an approach to an incarnate devil as can well
be imagined. If this were not the case, the whole story could
not have happened. He was a man who had revelled in
crime, till it had ceased to have even a pleasurable excitement for him, a wretch who had sated himself with vice,
until all but its most loathesome forms had lost their interest.
Such beings do perhaps exist. Count Cenci, as he lived, was
probably such a being; but in that case he was a monstrosity, and therefore no proper subject for artistic treatment.
An artist might as well paint a two-headed ox as a poet copy
such a moral enormity. But when he had once chosen his subject, the poet could not but paint him thus. The great crime
which armed the hand of his daughter, a beautiful and innocent girl, with a dagger to be used against her fathers life,
is only hinted at in the play before us, therefore his other
crimes must necessarily be exhibited in all their blackness.
Shelley might, it is true, have hinted at the steps by which
he sunk into such moral deformity. This he has not done,
and this is the great fault of the tragedy; but for it it would

be almost faultless. The character of Beatrice is wonderfully drawn, it is incomparably the best to be found in any English work of the age, both in conception and execution. In it Shelley excelled both Scott and Byron in their peculiar branches of art. Scott never drew a woman so perfectly. She has more than all the grace, womanliness, and dignity of his heroines. We feel that in the veins of this pure and gentle girl runs the blood of a hundred noble ancestors. We cannot point out the touches by which this effect is wrought, but they are there. She is more heroic, and yet more womanly than the most masterly of Scott's creations. A hundred little words and actions, even in the midst of her most fearful wrongs, betray her maidenly grace. On the other hand the fearful passion which hurries her on from despair to parricide, has all the power, and more than all the truth of Byron's highest flights. Lucretia is only less powerfully drawn than her daughter. The weakness of the broken spirited woman which is sometimes almost as strong as her love for her children and the shallownes of her mind, are well drawn and contrasted with the high intellect and firm will of Beatrice.

Adonais is a lament over the untimely death of John Keats, the poet whose works whe shall shortly have to examine. It is one of the best poems of the kind in our language, for Tennyson's In Memoriam is something more than a mere elegy. The imagery is grand and impressive, and the conclusion of the poem is one of the highest flights of imagination to be found in Shelley's works.

Epipsychidion is a very remarkable poem and it has had a considerable influence on our literature. In the form of a love-poem it embodies a long train of abstract thought; but it is a strange contrast to most philosophical poems. They are cold and dead, this glows with passion and is instinct with life. Thought has here become feeling, the purest and deepest feeling of the poet's soul.

The lyrical poems of Shelley are, as a rule, very happy.

9 *

The delicacy of his touch, and the music of his diction are better displayed in them than in any of his greater works. Those which are purely subjective are, for the most part, written in a tone of despondency, but they have none of Byrons exaggerated pathos. They express the poet's longing, his hope for a better and purer state of things than that which now exists, but no despair. He was cruelly persecuted, torn from the children he tenderly loved because of his opinions, banished from his family, deserted by his friends, and followed with a maniac hatred by people to whom he had done no wrong because he differed from the world on abstract questions, but he repaid evil with good, and spent his life in endeavours to benefit the race who thus cruelly persecuted him. In his subjective poems there is no bitternes, no hatred, no misanthropy. There is sometimes a deep sorrow and a still deeper pity. But decidedly the best of his lyrical poems are those produced by the influence of natural scenery.

In Italy Shelley became very intimate with Lord Byron, though that poet had but little sympathy with his pure and simple way of life, and his spiritual and rather wild theories. Boating was one of his favourite amusements. On the 8th of July 1822, when returning with Mr Williams from Leghorn, whither he had gone to welcome Leigh Hunt to Italy, his vessel was overtaken by a storm and sunk. All on board were drowned. When his body was washed on shore, Byron and Leigh Hunt burnt it there, and the heart and ashes were carried to Rome, and buried in the protestant cemetery. On his tomb were inscribed the words, „Cor Cordium".

In purely imaginative power Shelley was perhaps the first poet of his age. Buckle the most deeply read, and Macaulay the most brilliant of modern English historians agree in giving him that place. Macaulay says: „The strong imagination of Shelley made him an idolater in his own despite. Out of the most indefinite terms of a hard, cold, dark, metaphysical system he made a gorgeous Pantheon, full of beautiful, ma-

jestic, and life-like forms. He turned atheism itself into a
mythology, rich with visions as glorious as the gods that
live in the marble of Phidias or the virgin saints that smile
on us from the canvass of Murillo. The Spirit of Beauty,
the Principle of Good, the Principle of Evil, when he treated of them, ceased to be abstractions. They took shape and
colour. They were no longer mere words, but „intelligible
forms“, „fair humanities“, objects of love, of adoration, or
of fear. As there can be no stronger sign of a mind destitute
of the poetical faculty than that tendency which was so common among writers of the French school to turn images into
abstractions, Venus, for example, into Love, Minerva into
Wisdom, Mars into War, and Bachus into Festivity, so there
can be no stronger sign of a mind truly poetical than a disposition to reverse this abstracting process, and to make individuals out of generalities. Some of the metaphysical and
ethical theories of Shelley were certainly most absurd and per-
nicious ‚ But we doubt whether any modern poet has possessed
in an equal degree some of the highest qualities of the great
ancient masters. The words „bard“ and „inspiration“, which
seem so cold and affected when applied to other modern writers, have a perfect propriety when applied to him. He
was not an author, but a bard. His poetry seems not to
have been an art, but an inspiration. Had he lived to the
full age of man, he might not improbably have given to the
world some great work of the very highest rank in design
and execution.“ (Essay on Southey's edition of the Pil-
grims Progress.)

This statement seems to me to be correct. To Shelley all
nature seemed to be instinct with spirit. Hence came his
great love of the Greek mythology. To most men, even to
most poets, hill and vale, wood and meadow-land stand
simply for what they are. They may be used as imagery,
but, in that case, a conventional meaning is imparted to them.
To Shelley, even more than to Wordsworth, they seemed
to be but the dress in which some divine thought reveals or

hides itself. All nature seemed to him, to use the sublime
words of the greatest of modern poets, to be nothing but
the „Living garment of God". This belief which was in
Wordsworth nothing but an indistinct feeling, Shelley formed into a system. The atheism of his youth soon ripened into
a kind of spiritualized pantheism, the form of belief which
seems to have the greatest charm for young poets. This is
not the place to enter into an inquiry concerning the system
of philosophy which Shelley embraced, or rather constructed; but it is impossible to understand him if we do not remember that both his life and his works were embodiments
of that system. Shelley's poetry is often spoken of as a series
of splendid dreams, and so, for the most part, it is. Yet
no poet was ever more free of dreaminess in the common
sense of the word. His pictures are always sharp, his colours are always clearly marked. There is never a doubt as
to his meaning. The great fault of his poetry is its want of
reality, we feel that the beings he paints are too good, too
pure, too holy to tread this earth. Yet this is an after-
thought. When we read his poems, we do not doubt, indeed
in our higher hours we act, not only as if these things were
possible, but as if they were. The great moral doctrines of
Christianity: „Love those that hate you, bless them that curse
you, do good to them that dispitefully use you and persecute
you", never met with a higher illustration than in the life
and works of this young pantheist. The Cenci proves that
he was possessed of other, and perhaps rarer powers than
those which he has exhibited in most of his poems, that he
could, when he wished, write objectively and draw nature
as it really is. With respect to the lower poetical endow-
ments he was perhaps the most gifted poet of his age. His
diction is clearer and more nervous than that of any of his contemporaries. His command of language is marvellous. The melody of his verse surpasses that of any other modern English
poet except, perhaps, Tennyson. Moore and Coleridge are the
only writers of his age who can be compared with him in this

respect; but the latter poet has left too few examples of his power for us to place him in the same category, while Moore's forms are always more or less conventional. The same may be said of his imagery. Moore had always a „flower of fancy" ready to deck out any thought, but then they were generally cut and dried; we feel that the poet put them where they stand for the occasion, while Shelley's imagery seems to spring naturally from the soil on which it grows. One might as well compare a garland of artificial flowers with the luxurient blossoming of the woods in spring, as the best of Moore's poems with those of Shelley.

John Keats was born on the 29ᵗʰ of October 1795. He was educated at Enfield, and apprenticed to a surgeon in his fifteenth year. He devoted however the most of his time to literary studies. He published a volume of poems in 1817, and Endymion — a poetic romance — in the following year. This poem was bitterly attacked by Croker in the Quarterly review. Keats took this so much to heart that it embittered the rest of his short life and hastened, if it did not cause, the attack of consumption which terminated it. He died in Rome, whither he had gone as a last hope of saving his life, on the 27ᵗʰ of December 1820 shortly after completing his 25ᵗʰ year.

Keats seems to have been equally attracted by the imaginative literature of the middle ages and by the mythology of Greece and Rome. Of classical poetry he knew little; but the classical mythology, which he is said to have learnt from a mythological dictionary, made a deep impression on his mind. Hence the greatest of his poems are classical subjects treated in a romantic manner. It was not the first time that this experiment had been tried. The literature of all European countries, during the middle ages, furnish examples of this kind. Nowhere in our literature are such beauties and such defects to be found united in a single poem as in Endymion. The rhythm which seems to have been borrowed from the Faithful Shepherdess of Fletcher, was excellently suited to his

subject. The story of the poem has but little interest, he
did not intend it to have much, it was but the string with
which he bound together a garland of flowers. It is not the
fate of Endymion, but the beauties of nature, which he sings,
nor does he even endeavour to keep up a local colouring.
The land in which his hero dwells is a purely imaginary
country, but it resembles England much more than Greece.
„He has contrived", says Jefferies, „to impart to the whole
piece that true rural and poétical air which breathes only
in them (the pastoral poems of the Elizabethan age) and
Theocritus, which is at once homely and majestic, luxurious
and rude, and sets before us the genuine sights, sounds, and
smells of the country, with all the magic and grace of Elys-
ium. — The great distinction however between him and these
divine authors is that imagination in them is subordinate to
reason and judgement, while with him it is paramount and
supreme. Their ornaments and images were employed to em-
bellish and recommend just sentiments, engaging incidents,
and natural characters while his are poured out without mea-
sure and restraint and with no apparent design, but to un-
burden the breast of the author, and to give vent to the over-
flowing vein of fancy."

Isabella, a story versified from Boccacio, shows a great
advance in this respect, while St. Agnes Eve is perfect in its
way. In Hyperion, the last and finest of his poems, he returned to the old mythology. Byron said that it „seems actually inspired by the Titans, and is as sublime as Aeschylus."
The distance between Endymion and it is indeed vast, yet it
was traversed by the poet in less than two years. In the
latter poem all the beauties of the first are to be found, but
they are subjugated to a great plan, and it has a statuesque
beauty and repose which is wanting even in the greatest
works of the greatest of his contemporaries.

It is impossible to say what Keats might have become,
had he lived, we can only judge him by the works which
he has left behind him, but it would be unjust not to remem-

ber that they were written by a poet who died very young.
He occupies a very peculiar place in our literature. His
poems display no great power of expressing passion. He had
no talent for characteristic, nor any great depth of thought.
Yet his poetry is now very generally popular. He is the
poet of nature. He does not worship it as the embodiment
of the divine thought or life as Wordsworth and Shelley did,
he loves it for its own sake alone. But his love is not that
which comes of knowledge. It is the wild exuberant delight
that a young man, who has been long pent up in a city,
feels when he can escape for a week or two to the woods and
mountains; or rather, it resembles his winter remembrances
and dreams of such summer rambles. Every thing rural seems
bright to him, and he chooses the brightest and crowds them
on each other. We may indeed say that Scott idealized
natural scenes by giving only their characteristic lines, Byron
by illuminating them by the coloured light of subjective passion, Shelley by reproducing their internal entity, and Keats
by choosing their choicest beauties, and rearranging them to
a new whole. Keats's study of our old writers gave a mellow
fullness to his style, and a certain picturesqueness to his
diction, but in these respects he is far inferior to Shelley.

With Keats we must conclude our review of the poets of
this age. *Campbell* deserves mention for the force and careful polish of his verses, and *Crabbe* for his truthful delinea-
tion of life. The latter poet was however deficient in ideality.

Walter Savage Landor is a writer of vast powers and
great originality, but, differing widely from the popular writers of his age and country, and standing above them in
many respects, he has never become popular. His diction is
clear and forcible, but his favourite subjects have but little interest for most Englishmen. Indeed he is the least English
of all our great writers. Hence he is much less known than
he ought to be. No prose work of the age will bear a comparison with his Imaginary Conversations, in vigor, origina-

lity, and depth of thought. It is true that some of his opinions are very startling and eccentric, but there can be no
doubt that he deserves a high place among the prose writers
of his age. Much has been said both for and against his
poetry, some ranking it very high, and others placing it far
below his prose works. Here too his taste was opposed to
that of most of his contemporaries. His Count Julian is a
poem of great power. The situation is striking and the characters are well developed but the dramatical element is wanting. Gebir, his longest poem, was originally written in latin, and many of his smaller poems are imitations of the classics. It was the misfortune of Landor that he never could
find a form of expression which suited the taste of the public.
Perhaps he did not even endeavour to do so, but was content to write for a small but select circle. By these he is
enthusiastically admired, and his works are doubtless more
exquisitely finished, and better expressions of his genius than
they would have been had he conformed to the taste of the day.

Charles Lamb is another writer who will always be admired by a few highly refined minds, yet never widely popular. This is however the only characteristic which he has
in common with Walter Savage Landor. He was one of those
men whom we occasionally meet in England and America,
and who seem to have been placed there by some caprice of
nature, for the sake of contrast. The chief characteristic of
his life and writings is, as De Quincey has observed, their
thorough unworldliness. In delicacy and richness of humour
the „Essays of Elia" have never been equalled. Yet they
are not merely humourous. They contain passages of tender
pathos which are perhaps even more attractive. It is the
union of these qualities with a strange picturesque quaintness,
and a sensitively exact observation of those sides of human
life which are least treated by artists, that give these Essays
their indescribable charm.

B O O K III.

1832 — 1860.

Chapter I.

Our own age differs widely from that which we have just been considering. Seldom has any nation produced at once such a number of great poets as England could boast of at the commencement of our century. In our own age we shall find few indeed who can compare with them. But our prose literature has gained all, and more than all that our poetry has lost. Our own times seem to be more than any other the age of novels, and if the first years of this century gave birth to Byron, Scott, Wordsworth, and Shelley, the last thirty years can point with pride to Thackeray, Dickens, Trollope, Kingsley, and George Eliot. Our essayists too have increased in number, and have improved incalculably both in originality and depth of thought. From 1800 to 1832 our critical literature was unjust and superficial in the highest degree. As a natural consequence it was unprecedentedly severe. Now it would be difficult to find a critical literature which is, as a rule, more mild and just in its judgments than our own. Formerly every book was looked at from a party point of view. The political opinion of the author was a matter of more importance to the reviewer than the value of the book. Hence the Edinburgh and Quarterly reviews seldom agreed as to the value of a poem or novel that was not written by a well known author. Now no one thinks of enquiring whither a writer is Whig or Tory, monarchical or republican, unless he treats subjects closely connected with party questions. The tone of our critics too is much more

polished and gentlemanly than it was. Articles which formerly
appeared in the leading critical journals would not now be
published by any paper which has any pretension to be considered respectable. But the most hopeful sign for the future is perhaps the healthy moral tone of the literature of
our age. The captious discontent with men and things which
pervaded Byron's poetry fortunately passed away shortly after
his death, and Shelley's overstrained idealism found no imi-
tator.

In poetry, we find that the influence of Wordsworth and
Shelley has been more permanent than that of any of their
contemporaries. Hence reflective and lyrical poems are much
more common in our age than dramatic or narrative ones.
I endeavoured in a former chapter to point out the causes
of the decay of our drama. It is much easier to find the causes of narrative poetry being abandoned. The prose novel has
taken possession of a great part of the ground which was formerly occupied by poetical fiction. Before the time of Sir
Walter Scott all novels of note were either humourous stories,
or mere sentimental love - tales. Masterpieces of both kinds
had been written in England. Tristram Shandy and Clarissa
will never be surpassed in their own style. A few novelists,
among whom Fielding was the greatest master, united both
styles with wonderful success. Tom Jones, the best work of this
kind, still remains one of the greatest of English novels and
will bear a comparison even with the masterpieces of Cervan-
tes. Yet no one who is acquainted with our novel literature
before the time of Scott will wonder that serious and religious
people objected to it, and that it was forbidden ground for
the young. It was either worldly and sensual, or mawkishly
sentimental. The first of these faults is not to be wondered
at, it was intended for men only. Rousseau said that no
chaste girl ever read a novel, and this was certainly as true
of Engand as of France in those days. This being the case
writers spoke freely. There is nothing immoral in Fielding

and Sterne, but they called bad things by their worst names. Richardson and his followers, on the other hand, fell into the opposite extreme of sentimentality, and the tone of his tales is far more unhealthy than that of his less scrupulous contemporaries. As soon as ladies began to take an interest in literature, its tone improved; but, down to the time of Scott, no great master appeared who was able to win for the new kind of novel a permanent place in our literature. He entered an entirely new ground, for the works of Miss Porter scarcely deserve mention. He treated in his prose romances subjects which had before belonged almost exclusively to the drama. The characters he introduced were heroic, and he touched on all feelings by turn. Since his time, it is true, the novel has returned to the real life of our own age, but, through his influence, it embraces a much wider range of character and feeling. Every thing that can happen in our days, from the election of a dissenting minister and the troubles of a young wife who is ignorant of house - keeping to the death of a hero on the field of battle, is looked upon as a legitimate subject for a novel. Still more important has been the influence of German literature and particularly of Goethe's novels. Among these Wilhelm Meister has had the greatest and most beneficial influence. The interest of that tale is concentrated on the development of the heroes character. He undergoes an entire change during the progress of the story, and it is on this change that our attention is fixed. Other writers had tried to do this before, but never with any marked and permanent success. To the greatest of modern poets belongs the praise of first showing what novel-writing might become. In England he has found in Thackeray and George Eliot followers of whom even he would have no cause to be ashamed. This kind of writing has reacted on the historical novel. The interest of the best works of this kind is now no longer centred on external and accidental circumstances, but on the characters of the people introduced.

The scene is no longer laid in distant lands and ages because wild adventure will seem less improbable there than in the midst of England in the nineteenth century, but because strange circumstances gave birth to strange characters, and these interest the novelist. This is what raises George Eliot's Romola so immeasurably above the best of the Waverley novels. In the mean time the literature of France has had a great, though by no means so great an influence upon this branch of writing. Unfortunately the moral tone of Balzac's writings has prevented them having so wide an influence on our novel-writers as the amazing genius of that strangely cynical author entitled him to. Single English authors have learnt much from him, but his influence has not been wide. This is to be regretted, for, spite of his many faults, he is probably the greatest analyzer of human nature and character who ever lived. Unhealthy imitations of sensational French stories have unfortunaltely become popular of late among our third-rate authors and authoresses, but they hardly fall either in time or character within the scope of our present sketch. French influence has been most felt in the class of tales that are generally known as „novels with a purpose". The poetical and delicately wrought tales in which George Sand teaches her novel social theories have given birth in England to a number of stories which are neither poetical nor delicately wrought, and to a few books of real power. But no English work of this kind can be compared to the best writings of that gifted authoress. The influence of the Danish poet Andersen's shorter tales is to be traced in many of our best writers, but rather in increasing the healthiness of their general tone, and in sharpening their powers of observation than by any particular bent which he has given their stories. — This slight sketch shows that our novelists have learned much from foreign writers, but no one will doubt that, spite of this, they are strikingly original. They have not merely gathered scraps of foreign riches together; they have moulded foreign materials into new shapes, or used foreign tools in shaping English subjects. Intercourse of this kind widens and enriches a literature, while mere imitation narrows and impoverishes it.

It would be both interesting and instructive to enter into a detailed examination of the effects of periodical writing on our novels, but we can only note a few of the most important signs of that influence. Periodical literature has increased, during our age, in an extraordinary degree. Magazines or miscellanies of some kind are to be found in every drawing room, and in almost every kitchen. Most of these papers are of course mere trash, but some of them are very powerfully written. These papers have superseded the novels in monthly parts which had a great run at the commencement of our period. All our great novelists have contributed to one or other of them, and a vast number of tales are written for them alone. Hence their influence on this branch of our literature has been vast. Perhaps George Eliot is the only one of our first class novelists who has entirely escaped from it, and this is probably the case only because she is too consummate an artist to publish any part of a novel before the whole is completed. But it is on our third and fourth class writers that the effects have been most injurious. A good magazine tale must at once awaken interest, and it is easier to do this by some horrible crime, unnatural action or great mystery than by a careful development of character. Hence our sensational novels, the worst and most unhealthy of all works of imagination, have arisen. To the same cause the mannerism of many even of our better writers may be attributed. A periodical writer must be striking if he is to be successful, and peculiarities are striking. Hence a number of our authors have cultivated a peculiar style of expression which has a superficial appearance of originality — that false god of talented young men. All great poets are original, but they aim at truth rather than originality. Shakespeare and

Goethe are the most original of modern writers, but they never endeavoured to be so. They asked what is true and beautiful, not what is new and strange. Their diction is simple and idiomatic, not peculiar and startling. Indeed there can be no surer sign of the want of the highest genius than an artificial mannerism. Again, an author who offers his works in short parts to the public must except it to work in parts rather than as a whole; hence comes the want of artistic unity which is to be found in many even of our best works of fiction. This is to be remarked in a faulty construction of the plot which is so observable even in the writings of some of our best novelists. But with all these faults some advantages at least have resulted from the system of periodical writing. The liveliness of the novel has been increased, and dullness — the one unforgivable sin of such books — has certainly decreased. Still we cannot but regret that the more talented of our novelists should not have an opportunity of reviewing and correcting their works after they are finished; we cannot but see that many of the faults which deface them would in that case have been removed.

On turning to our essayists we find that most men who have exercised any great influence on our age belong, at least in some degree, to this class, but their subjects and way of writing differ so widely that it is difficult to say in which direction this branch of our literature is tending. Thomas Carlyle is perhaps the essayist who has had the widest and deepest influence, both for good and evil, on the minds of his contemporaries. There is scarcely a single branch of study, except the natural sciences, in which it is unfelt. In our theology, our poetry, our criticism, and our novel writing the influence of this eccentric thinker is clearly to be traced. For the most part the effects of his writings have been beneficial. They have deepened the feelings, and extended the sympathies of our writers. They have made their works more sincere and manly, but his deification of mere brute force and the eccentricity of his style can scarcely be said to deserve praise.

One of the most unmixed benefits which Carlyle has conferred upon us is the attentive study of the German literature which his early essays did much to promote. Being himself an enthusiastic admirer of Goethe, he called the attention of his countrymen to the works of that great poet and several other German writers. He has translated Wilhelm Meister, and the Märchen, and written a life of Schiller. To his influence too must be attributed, at least in part, the fact that the knowledge of German instead of being, as it was in the last age, an accomplishment which was confined to a few scholars, is now considered a necessary part of a liberal English education.

CHAPTER II.

Alfred Tennyson is, beyond all doubt, the greatest poet of our age. His first volume of poems was published in the year 1830. These poems were principally distinguished by their unreality. Their subjects were as far removed from common every-day life as possible. In this they resembled Shelley's poems, but they for the most part wanted the earnestness and enthusiasm which made even the wildest of his dreams seem almost possible and true. Most of these verses were wild flights of fancy, the dreams of an imagination luxuriating in all that is sweetest in nature. The verses were melodious, more melodious perhaps than those of any modern English poet, the diction was chaste beyond all comparison, and the pictures were beautiful in the highest degree; but it was the beauty of a butterfly, the music of a birds song, wild and sweet, but without meaning or power to stir the

10 *

higher part of man's nature. I speak only of the majority
of the poems, the exceptions I shall mention farther on.
Depth of thought and feeling seemed all that was wanting to
give the young poet a high place in our literature. But unfortunately the only poem in which he tried to delineate
passion was weak and powerless. Oriana wanted even the
charms of music and expression which seemed so peculiarly
Tennyson's own. Yet Mariana proved that the poet had
powers of a very high and original order, and that he could
paint with delicacy some mental moods. In it he endeavours
to delineate the feelings of a girl who has lost her lover. It
is not the passionate agony of loss, but the utter weariness
of life which succeeds such anguish that forms the subject of
the poem. We feel that it is this state of mind that casts
its shadow over the whole landscape around, which might
else be beautiful but which is now so intolerably dreary.
Several of the poems contained in this volume were headed
by the names of ladies, but they were not love-poems.
They were fanciful and imaginative trains of thought and
feeling suggested by different kinds of beauty. Sunny dreams,
it is true, but, as passionless as if they had been adressed to
a bird or a flower.

Emerson thus criticised these earlier poems. „Tennyson
is endowed precisely in points where Wordsworth wanted.
There is no finer ear, nor more command of the keys of
language. Colour, like the dawn, flows over the horizon
from his pencil, in waves so rich that we do not miss the cen-
tral form. Through all his refinements, too, he has reached
the public — a certificate of good sense and general power,
since he who aspires to be the English poet must be as large
as London, not in the same kind as London but in his own
kind. But he wants a subject and climbs no mount of vision to bring its secrets to the people. He contents himself
with describing the Englishman as he is, and proposes no
better. There are all degrees in poetry; and we must be

thankful for every beautiful talent. But it is only a first success, when the car is gained. The best office of the best poets has been to show how low and uninspired was their general style, and that only once or twice they have struck the high chord."

In 1832 Tennyson published a second volume. It rather disappointed the admirers of the first. The wild music of the rhythm was less apparent. The author seemed to have laid aside his Shelley and studied Wordsworth instead. He was right in doing so. His poems had gained in depth and power. Here we find Tennyson's first published attempts at forms of writing in which he afterwards most excelled. Leaving the Lady of Shallot, a narative poem closely connected with the story of King Arthur, we come to the Miller's Daughter, and the May Queen. The first of these is an idyllic poem, but it differs widely from Burns's Saturday-night and other poems of the same kind. The beauties and pleasures of rustic life are painted here, it is true, but they are painted by a dreamy and highly refined observer, not in the manner of a rustic. The May Queen is a delicately penciled sketch of a village-girl's life. It shows a great fineness of touch, and a power of appreciating the moments of a mental struggle. The Pallace of Art is much praised, and it is a piece of finely wrought description. It is an allegorical history of a refined mind which, by separating itself from human interests, becomes diseased, a poetical attempt to prove that beauty alone is as incapable of satisfying man's higher nature as truth alone. I must confess it is no great favourite of mine. The finest poem in the volume, in my opinion one of the finest Tennyson has ever written, is The Dream of Fair Women. Here his wonderful plastic talent, his exquisite taste, and his power of delineating the dreamy and evanescent shades of human thought and feeling have full play, while the subject does not demand the realism and force which he possesses in a less degree. The diction

and rhythm of the piece are perfect. The poet falls asleep
over Chaucer's Legend of good women, and that wonderful
romance weaves itself into his dream. He finds himself alone
in a vast forest. Here he meets and holds converse with
the „far renowned brides of ancient song". Their different
characters are drawn and contrasted with great power. This
is a good specimen of one of Tennyson's favourite manners.
He loves to draw characters half subjectively and half objectively, to give rather the picture they leave on his own
mind, than their real characters. Hence the outline is generally true to nature, but it is filled up with little subjective
touches.

Tennyson's English Idylls would repay an attentive study,
did the space permit us to examine them closely; as it is, we
must pass hastily over them. Dora is the nearest approach to a
true Idyll that Tennyson has ever made. The diction and
manner of treatment are simple in the extreme. The characters too are well drawn and contrasted. It is far superior
to any of Wordsworth's poems of the same kind. St. Simeon
Stylites betrays however a far greater and more original
power. It purports to be the last prayer of that extraordinary man who, by a self appointed penance, passed his life on
the top of a column. Tennyson delights in describing states of
mind in which various and often opposite feelings come into
play. A simple soul-absorbing passion he cannot paint with any
great power; but in describing complex emotion he surpasses all
our modern poets except Browning. This is perhaps the most
extraordinary proof of this power which he has given. The
unhealthy and overstrained ideality, and the sincere religiousness, which must have formed the ground-work of such a
character, are modified and tinted by the vanity which seems
to be just as necessary a part of a martyr's constitution. The
mingled pride and humility with which he dwells on his sins
are drawn by a few simple and masterly touches; but after

all this piece is rather a poetical study of character than a poem. Love and Duty, though a less powerful sketch, is a better poem. Here too a complex mood of mind is described. It is thought coloured by feeling, or rather penetrated and animated by it. It is perhaps the most passionate piece the poet has ever written.

His next poem, The Princess a Medley, is a remarkable work. The tale is as wild and improbable as a dream, but it is finished with exquisite delicacy. The characters too are well drawn and true to nature, though they are removed from common life as far as possible. The golden light of romance is cast upon them. Though the clearness of outline is never lost, they never seem to be quite real. Yet the book contains the poet's ideas on one of the great social questions of the day, „woman's mission". This is the thread that binds it to every day life. Almost every scene would furnish a good picture, and Tennyson's wonderful plastic power gives to each something of the effect of a painting. It is interesting to compare his writings with those of Sir Walter Scott in this respect. The two poets seem to have nothing in common. Scott's power lies in the firmness of his lines, and what artists call the massing of his colouring. He has something of the dash of Rubens. He loves striking contrasts. Every thing in his writings speaks of power. Each incident or trait of character has its own purpose, and it is easy to see what that purpose is. Tennyson is in these respects a perfect contrast to him. His power is far more subtle. It depends on the delicacy of the touches and the tone of his pictures. He delights in exquisite finish and perfect harmony. His incidents have often a meaning which is at first quite unapparent, but which is necessary to the effect of the whole. It is very difficult to analyze the effect of his poetry. It is generally easy to point out the leading traits of Scott's tales, and to say what influence each has on the general impression left on the mind of the reader. With Tennyson it is very difficult to do this. The whole tale is raised and idealized by an indefinable process. There rests both on his landscapes and incidents a light that never was on earth and sea. We cannot discover why lines and passages of his poems move us as they do. Much of this is doubtless owing to the perfection of his rhythmical forms which are in all his finer poems faultless. Much too must be ascribed to his diction. Not only is it more chaste and idiomatic than that of any English poet since the Elizabethan age, it is also highly suggestive. His words hint far more than they say. To the uninitiated they seem simple and common-place, over those who are acquainted with our ancient literature they have a strange power. The more one reads of the old romances, the more one studies Chaucer and our great dramatists, the more one learns to admire the poems of Tennyson. His verses like charms have a mystic significance. They have the power of summoning up a thousand remembrances. Change but a word and this power is lost. The Princess contains some of the most musical of Tennyson's lyrical poems.

In Memoriam is professedly a lament over the death of Arthur Hallam, the son of the historian and critic. But it is something much more than this, or it could never have attained the vast popularity it enjoys among the most earnest and refined Englishmen of the age. To many it came like a new gospel comforting and strengthening. By these it has doubtless been overvalued. I doubt if it will be numbered among the greatest of Tennyson's poems in a hundred years time, and I do not think it will ever be much read out of England. It is very difficult to find a class of poems to which it can be said to belong. It resembles in many respects the philosophical poem, but it differs from other works of this class in being rather the description and expression of a series of mental moods than the exponent of a system. The various theories that are started in it are introduced rather on account of their influence on the feelings of the author than for their intrinsic value. They are the means but not the end of the poet.

I have already spoken of Tennyson's talent for describing complex moods of mind, of his power of tracing the influence of thought on feeling and feeling on thought. In Memoriam is a new example of this power. It is no mere expression of grief at the loss of a friend, though no poem of the kind in our language speaks of such love and such sadness, or carries with it such an impress of sincerity. The grief is coloured and modified by the whole train of the poet's thought. To understand this poem aright, we must bear in mind one great difference between England and Germany. England is orthodox and Germany freethinking. Here theology is a question of purely scientific interest. The character and life of Jesus, and the nature of the relationship between the human soul and God can be discussed as coolly as a question in natural science, and much more coolly than a political theory. In England the case in vastly different. Religious thought colours and levens society. It influences the life of most men, and is the chief occupation of many. It is the one question which transcends the common business of every day, that excites the interest of all. This feeling may often be distorted, it may sink into superstition and hypocrisy, but after all it is the salt of English society. It prevents our national life from putrefying and becoming a mass of corruption. It is the poetical element that dignifies, and enobles the labours of the poor and casts upon the petty cares of every day an ideal glory. Nor is this state of things getting rarer. Every one who is acquainted with our imaginative writings must have noticed that religious questions now influence the higher branches of our literature much more than they have ever before done. Now when theological doubt enters into a mind which has been educated under

these influences, it is obvious that it cannot be treated
as a merely scientific question.   It is not a theory that is
threatened, it is the principle of a life that has to be overthrown.   The first hours of doubt are to such a mind the
deepest anguish the heart of man can conceive.   The glory
seems to have departed from life.   All that lent beauty and
grandeur to existence is gone.   This is the key to much that
seems incomprehensible to foreigners in the intellectual life
of England.   It explains the untenable theories which so
many otherwise talented men have endeavoured to defend,
as drowning men catch at straws.   It accounts too for the
strange fact that intellectual scepticism is often with us the
first step to dissoluteness.   Two very remarkable books aim
at expressing and embodying the struggle with doubt through
which as a baptism of fire most of our earnest men have had
to pass.   The one is Carlyle's Sartor Resartus, the other is
Tennyson's In Memoriam.

Maud was the name of his next poem.   It is a story,
or rather a picture of the feelings and development of a very
morbid mind, told in a series of semi-lyrical poems.   Some
passages are among the finest Tennyson ever wrote.

In 1849 the Idylls of the King were published.   This work,
taken as a whole, is perhaps his masterpiece.   It consists
of four stories, taken from the myth of Arthur and the Knights
of the Round Table.   This subject had early been familiar to
his mind.   In his second volume he had treated a part of it
in The Lady of Shallot, a poem with the same subject as
Elaine.   Again, in his English Idylls, there is a poem on
the death of Arthur which might have been placed at the end
of the volume we are now examining, so closely does it resemble it in spirit and treatment.   Nor can we wonder at Tennyson's love for this story.   It is perhaps the highest embodiment of the spirit of the middle ages.   The tale, it is true,
has never been embodied in a poem that can be compared to
the Nibelungenlied, but the story seems to me to have been

susceptable of a far higher treatment. The Nibelungenlied too bears many traces of its heathen origin, while the tale of Arthur and the search for the Holy Graal is thorough- ly Christian and chivalrous, .and is therefore a better expression of a thoroughly Christian and chivalrous age. There was much in the nature of the story to attract Tenny- son. The scene was laid in a distant age, so that it had the dim mellowness of antiquity in which he delights, but the period is so uncertain, so perfectly mythical, that it needed none of the minute details which would have been necessary in an historical subject. His imagination had free scope. He might mould the tale according to his fancy, and fill it with modern ideas and trains of thought. He made free use of this power, with what success we shall presently see. The first great difference between .the old romance - writers and Tennyson is to be found in the character of Arthur. I cannot of course enter into a detailed examination of the story, it belongs to the middle ages and not to the nine- teenth century. I may remark however that in the old story the king is guilty of a great crime which renders all his work vain. This crime can never be forgiven, at least in this world, and he, and the goodly fellowship of the Round Table, are doomed to fall by the same sin which he in his youth committed. This lends a certain grandeur and dignity to his fate. His fall is not accidental, it is necessary and tragical, for here, once again, the devine might of law is asserted. Vain is Arthur's penance,. vain his knightly skill and high endeavour, the devine law has been broken and must be avenged. In Tennyson's hands this grandly tragical character, with his great sin and his still greater penance, becomes a perfect knight and spotless king. His guilt is wiped away, he becomes a sinless man struggling for a high, but impossible end. Morally he has doubtless gained much by the change; aesthetically he seems to me to have lost im- measurably. His story has become a mere domestic tragedy.

The sin of Lancelot and Guinevere too becomes much darker
in the reader's eyes.   When reading the best of the old romances we feel that they have been guilty of a great sin,
but we feel at the same time that they have been forced
into it by fate.   Thus, without the tragical guilt being les-
sened, the heroes are half excused in our eyes.   But the
greatest evil which arises from this alteration is that it renders it impossible for Tennyson to treat the search for the
San Graal, which is by far the grandest part of the story.
For, if the king had been spotless, he must have won the
holiest of relics, and then the last part of the story becomes impossible.   We cannot examine all the points of
difference between the ancient and modern version of the
story; one more must suffice.   Merlin is the great sorcerer
of Arthur's court.   He was, according to the old story, the
wisest of men.   He knew every thought that entered into
a man's heart.   Yet, according to the myth, he is cheated
by a woman into telling her a charm with which she binds
and imprisons him.   Here is a great difficulty.   The wisest
of men has to be duped.   The old romance-writers meet the
difficulty honestly.   They represent Merlin as a Titanic character, a man who was not only infinitely wiser than other
men, but infinitely greater in every respect, a being of unbounded intellect, but also of unbounded passion, a man
who excelled his fellows in love as much as in knowledge.
This Merlin meets the wisest of women, and loves her with
the whole depth of his nature.   He teaches her all that he
knows, and at last he becomes the slave, he is never the
dupe, of his passion.   He leaves the court of Arthur knowing that he shall never return to it again, and at last he tells
the secret charm, although he knows that it will be used to
imprison him, because he cannot refuse her anything she
asks.   „So he taught her the charm", says one of the old
romances, „and on this account he has always been considered a fool, even to this day, but he could not help

himself, he was forced to do it". The reason why she wove
the charm about him was that she feared that he might grow
tired of her, if not, was not her company enough for him?
Tennyson changes Merlin into a doting old man, and Vivien
into a heartless flirt, who imprisons him only to show her
power. In short the passionate romance becomes, in his
hand, a warning to old men to beware of young ladies.
This version of the story is doubtless to be found in the literature of the middle ages, but when he had the choice between two such tales, there can., I think, be little doubt
as to which he should have taken. Still, whatever may be
their faults, the Idylls of the King are Tennyson's greatest
poems, the best verses which have been written in England
in our age.

It is interesting to compare Elaine with the Lady of Shallot, an earlier poem of Tennyson's which I have already mentioned. In both poems the conclusion is the same, and it was
probably this conclusion which induced the poet to choose the
subject. The scene is striking and picturesque. A boat, con-
taining the dead body of a young and beautiful girl, floats at
midnight into Camelot, where Arthur and his knights are re-
velling. This is the end of both pieces, but it is all they have
in common. The rest of the poems are good specimens of Tennyson's earlier and later styles. The Lady of Shallot is a
beautiful poem, but it is entirely without human interest. Its
heroine is a lady, who is forced by enchantment to embroider
something or another, and who falls under the power of the spell
as soon as she ceases to do so. The heroine of Elaine is a
simple girl who sees Lancelot and falls in love with him,
and tends him when wounded and dies. It is a simple and
beautiful love-tale, simply and tenderly told, impossible if
you like in our days, but not among the heroic figures which
crowd the story of Arthur. The conclusion is not only more
picturesque than that of the earlier story, it is far more tender and pathetic. Tennyson too has given it, by its position

in the Idylls of the King, a second and very deep significance. The dead Elaine comes to Lancelot as he is quarelling
with Guinivere. She comes as is if she were indeed a mes-
senger from the land of the dead to warn him to break from
the unholy passion that binds him. Her silence speaks louder than any voice, but it speaks in vain. Elaine, in death
as in life, passes unheeded and yet she is Lancelot's good
angel. After she is buried and forgotten, we pass on at
once to the tragical end of the story, over which we cannot
linger. — In comparing the Idylls of the King with the ancient myth, I have pointed out one or two points in which,
as it seems to me, Tennyson's version is inferior to that of
the middle ages. It is but justice to add that his poem is by
far the best that has been written in English on the subject.
None of our metrical romances will bear a comparison with
it. They are, for the most part, at once rude and fanciful.
They attract by their matter rather than their form. Some
of them, it is true, contain passages of exquisite beauty,
but they are almost all deformed by tasteless inventions and
wearisome episodes. They exhibit a high creative power,
but this power is too often misapplied. It knows neither li-
mit nor restraint. Indeed, it seems as if our ancient romance-
writers were the foolish retellers of a glorious tale which
they themselves could only imperfectly understand. They
dwell on unimportant details and pass carelessly over grand
situations. Their writings appear to be imperfect and ill
painted copies of a grand original. We are startled every
now and then by splendid conceptions which are never realized, by hints of a grandeur which is never expressed.
Tennyson has realized the conception. He has freed the
grand idea of the myth from the adventures that uselessly
encumbered it. He has introduced a unity into the tales he
has told. Above all, he has always kept in mind the ethical
ground-work of the tale. When we turn from the Idylls of
the king to the stories on which they are based, we are ama-

zed at the difference of their moral tone. The old poems are
licentious and ascetic by turns. Their writers perpetually
forget the principles without which their stories are incomprehensible. I am no stickler of morality in works of art.
I have no wish to make poetry the mere gilding of a moral
pill, nor to see our literature reduced to a series of tales for
little girls. But there are principles without which art cannot exist any more than society. The artist is at liberty to
choose his principles, but having chosen them, he must be
true to them. I cannot pretend to be shocked at the immorality of Congreve and Fielding. The tone of their works
is the same from beginning to end, and we can resign ourselves to the imagination of the author. He has created a
world which is governed by other laws than ours, and we
can submit to its laws. How far such a literature is injurious to public morality, is a question for the moralist and
not for the critic. But the case is otherwise with our metrical romances. If guilty love be not a great crime, whence
comes the tragic pathos of the conclusion of the story? Tennyson has always remembered this, and this is one of the
things which make the Idylls of the King so much superior
to the ancient poems on the subject as a work of art. It is
needless to speak of the delicacy with which the poet has
painted his characters and situations, of the chasteness of
his diction, and the music of his verse; but we must dwell
one moment on his historic truth, as this is one of the sides
on which the poem has been attacked. A society like his
court of Arthur, with its noble courtesy and valour, never,
of course, existed. In it the poet gives us a picture of the
ideal of chivalry, and, in so doing, he follows the example
of the greatest poets of the middle ages. „But", it is said,
„his picture·would have been quite incomprehensible to the
old knights. It is o u r ideal of chivalry that he paints, not
t h e i r s". There is some truth in this, though less than
there seems to be at the first glance. Many of the traits

which are pointed out as modern are to be found in the
works from which he drew his tales, but there can be n₁
doubt that, as a whole, his code of morals is at once less
fanciful and less barbarous than that which any poet of the
middle ages would have drawn. His knights are more broadly
human than any of their heroes. But is this a fault? I
think not. The end which the poet has to aim at is the
creation of beauty, not the exact reproduction of the past.
Even when he draws his materials from history, he has a
right to remodel his subject as it may seem best to him. The
greatest poets have always done this. Shakespeare was no
antiquarian, and every reader of Egmont knows how careless Goethe was of historical accuracy. The very thing that
some critics have blamed is perhaps the highest proof of
Tennyson's poetical genius which the work furnishes. To
reproduce the ideal of the middle ages is comparatively easy;
but to render that ideal comprehensible to people who live
in a state of society so widely different from the feudal times
as our own, is a task which only a poet of a high order
could have executed. Had the poet been content to follow
the old romance-writers in this respect, he might have exhibited a vast amount of curious reading, but he would have
produced a very inferior poem.

Enoch Arden, the last of Tennyson's poems, was published in 1864. The greater part of the poems contained in
this volume do not require any very close examination. They
resemble the English Idylls in manner and subject. The
Nothern Farmer however shows that Tennyson possesses
talents which he has never before exhibited. This prejudiced
and one-sided, but still powerful and vigorous character is
sketched with great force.

The poetry of Tennyson will probably never be popular in
the sense in which Burns's songs are popular. His verses will
never be sung by peasants and fishermen. His poems are too
finely wrought, his genius is too delicate, his intellect too subtle

to make any deep impression on the minds of the uneducated. His poetry is the product of a high state of culture. Its beauties can only be appreciated by men of such mental refinement as is seldom to be found except in those whose taste has been educated by the study of the masterpieces of poetical art. He never dazzles by gaudy colouring, nor attracts by rhetorical display. His very rhythm, the most melodious to be found in our literature, is too exquisitely toned to suit the taste of the crowd. From this it has most unjustly been argued that he is a poet rather by study than nature. Art, say these critics, is the universal language of mankind. It appeals to the broadly human part in our nature and is therefore universally comprehensible. The poet who is incomprehensible to any large body of his countrymen is, by his own confession, a poet of a low order. There is some truth in this theory, but the above statement of it is far too sweeping, and it is most unjust to judge Tennyson by it. It would make the opinion of the lowest orders the criterion of taste. Judged by it, Pierce Egan would be a greater novelist than George Eliot, and Schiller a greater poet than Goethe. In painting and music the application of it would be even more absurd. The lower classes would prefer the worst daub to be found in the gallery to [the grandest work of Michael Angelo or Raphael. They cannot enjoy Don Juan or Fidelio, but the Bohemian Girl delights them. In a word, it is evident that some amount of intellectual culture is necessary to enable the mind to enjoy the highest art. A few men of genius of the highest order have, it is true, been able to attract at once the refined and the uneducated, but they have succeeded only by the union of different, and even dissimilar qualities. It is not the power of characteristic, the truth to nature, the poetical beauty or the depth of thought which the gallery admires in a Shakespearean piece, but the clash of swords, and the pomp of the spectacle. The highest beauties of Shakespeare and Goethe make absolutely no impres-

sion on the uneducated, even when they go to see Hamlet
and Faust. No one thinks of placing Tennyson beside those
great masters. He himself would be the first to protest
against so foolish a comparison. But it is unjust to deny
that an author whose works are a source of deep and conti-
nuous enjoyment to the greatest of his countrymen is a poet
of a high order, because his poems are not read by the lowest
and least educated.

The earlier poems of Tennyson were, as we have seen,
wanting in human interest. The criticism of Emerson had
some justice when applied to them; but this is not the case
with his later works. We have lingered so long over his
various writings that it is now only necessary to add a few
words as to their general character. Faultless taste is one
of their highest merits. It is this which has kept the author
from thrusting himself before the public as Byron delighted
to do, and the fact that our poetry has been freed from the
egotistical vanity of his followers, is in a great degree owing to Tennyson's influence. Another fault from which his
later poems are entirely free is metrical trickery. A perfect
master of all rhythmical forms, he never writes merely to
show his mastery. The rhythm in his works is, as it always
should be, the form of the thought, not a clever contrivance
to hide the absence of thought. In his last volume, it is
true, he has inserted a series of metrical experiments, but
they were intended to have rather a scientific than an artistic interest. The same work contains one or two poems
which the poet would, in my opinion, have done well to
suppress, as their querulous impatience of criticism is hardly
worthy of a man who stands at the head of our literature,
and their tone approaches that egotism which it is one of his
greatest merits to have avoided.

Mrs *Browning* is probably, next to Tennyson, the most
popular of modern English poets. She is decidedly the greatest of our poetesses. Her poems want the polish of those

of Tennyson. They are sometimes harsh, and the diction is often obscure, but they are full of passion and force. They move the mind much more deeply than those of her great rival, but they move it differently. They remind us of the utterances of a prophetess who endeavours to speak what no human tongue can express. Now and then passages of wonderful power and terseness are to be found in her works. Every line, too, bears witness to the great passionate woman's heart that utters it.

Her political poems are the best verses of the kind which the present age has produced in England. They treat, for the most part, the modern history of Italy, in which country she spent the last years of her life. Some passages in Poems before Congress have certainly great poetical merit, whatever their political value may be. Her greatest work is Aurora Leigh, the history of the life of a poetess in blank verse. The story is wild and even incoherent in parts, yet taken as a whole, it is perhaps the greatest poetical work of our age. It certainly has a much deeper hold on our human sympathies than any of Tennyson's poems. The leading idea is the contrast between the ideal of the artist and that of the social reformer. Aurora Leigh is the representative of the one, Romney of the other. They are cousins, but they cannot comprehend though they love each other. Aurora, vexed at Romney's contempt for her ideals, and believing that he offers to marry her rather from pity of her poverty than from real affection, refuses his offer. They each go their own way, and each in time discovers that the choice has been onesided; that neither is perfect without the other. Such is a rough sketch of the plan. The whole work is saturated with original thought. One cannot read a page without chancing on some original and striking passage, and many grand and beautiful pictures. Indeed I do not know any modern English poem which presents so many new views of life in an equally small compass.

11 *

Robert Browning, the husband of the lady whose works
we have just been examining, possesses perhaps greater intellectual power than any poet of the day, yet he can hardly
be called the greatest of our living poets. His works are
strikingly original both in form and subject, but are they poetry? He is destitute of all the lower talents of a poet.
His verse is so harsh that it sometimes seems as if he were
endeavouring to write as discordantly as possible. His diction is so involved that the reader can hardly guess at the
meaning until he has read the piece through six or seven
times. Many of his works, too, are rather studies than
poems, but then they are such studies as no one else in our
age can execute. Robert Browning seems to look at all questions from a psychological point of view. He does not ask
what theory is true, but what is the logical connexion of
each theory, how is it possible to believe it true. No writer
has ever exhibited as clearly as he the relation of character
to opinion. He takes a given man, a spirit-rapper medium,
or a half sincere Catholic bishop for example, and evolves
his theory of the universe, and supports it by a thousand
arguments. You hear the man speak as he would really
speak, had he Mr Browning's learning and force of mind.
On the next page you have quite another character, a Hebrew prophet perhaps, and he tells you the secrets of his
soul. The poet contrasts their theories not with any moral
end, but simply from a love of artistic effect. „Are not all
systems equally good and bad" he seems to say „since they
are all indubitably the production of nature?" All souls
seem to lie open to his gaze. He can read the secrets of each,
the highest and the lowest, the enraptured saint and the
low impostor, he has fathomed them all. We may take his
poem Rabbi Ben Ezra for example. It breathes the very
spirit of the old Testament. It is an elaboration of the system
which gave utterance to the thought „Woe unto him that
striveth with his Maker; shall the clay say to him that fashion-

eth What makest Thou?" That frame of mind which looks
upon human beings as creatures fashioned by the Almighty
for his pleasure, and worth just what their value in his eyes
is, neither more nor less, is powerfully depicted. Perhaps no
mental state is more foreign to the thoughts and feelings of
our age than this resignation, this self-abnegation, yet Browning has expressed it in a most masterly manner. But though
he can paint a vast number of characters, he seldom gives us
more than a single side of each — the intellectual side; or
perhaps it would be more correct to say, he looks at most
of his characters from an intellectual point of view alone.
The other sides of his characters are, in the poems where
his originality is displayed to most advantage, only mentioned to show their influence on the intellect. Many of his lyrical poems prove that he can treat passion and emotion as
well. The simple pathos of some of these is very touching.
Take the following verse from his poem entitled „In a Year"

„Was it something said,
Something done
Vexed him, was it touch of hand,
Turn of head?
Strange that very way
Love begun,
I as little understand
Loves decay.

But it would be easier to find poets who could produce
such verses as the above than men who are capable of writing such poems as „Caliban on Setebos", or „Bishop Blou-
gram's apology." Mr Browning's dramas exhibit many of
the talents which are required in a great dramatist, a power
of grasping great situations, portraying characters, and expressing passion, but the theatrical element, the quality that
fits a play for the stage, is wanting in them.

The poetry of Browning, like that of Tennyson, but
for very different reasons, appeals to the educated alone.

He has neither the fine ear, nor the exquisite taste of the Laureate. His diction is involved, and we are sometimes startled by the introduction of colloquial phrases into his most serious poems. This often makes a grotesque, and sometimes even a comical impression. But these are not the qualitics,that prevent him becoming popular. The poetry of the people, be it narrative, dramatic or lyrical, always appeals to the feelings. Those poems which exhibit Mr Browning's powers to the greatest advantage appeal to the intellect. We seldom are inclined either to laugh or weep over his verses; yet we read and reread them, finding new beauties every time. But these beauties are apparent to the thinking alone. They consist of subtle trains of thought and striking views of life. His works are, as a rule, more remarkable for power than beauty. He scorns prettiness and prefers a forcible expression to a weak one even though it be less melodious. He is eccentric both in his choice of subjects and his manner of treating them. But he is a thinker of extraordinary depth and originality, a poet whose best works never loose their freshness and interest. The taste for his works, like that for olives and caviare, may be an acquired one, but it is a source of exquisite enjoyment.

Owen Meredith is the author of several volumes of poems which are very unequally written. The best of them deserve a very high place among the lyrics of our age. Tennyson has written but few poems that surpass „The Novel". But few of his verses are so well finished off, and many are careless in the extreme. The effect of Heine's writings may be traced in almost every thing he has written, except his religious or semi-religious pieces. Renaldo Renaldi is a mere translation of some chapters of the „Reisebilder" into English verse. The verses are spirited and would deserve great praise, had they been published as a translation or adaptation. The motives of several other poems he has borrowed without acknowledgements from the same source. Yet it would be

unjust not to give him credit for some originality. Now and
then he expresses a mental mood of mind with great power
and simplicity, take for example these verses from the Love-
Letter

But we are punished for our noblest deeds,
And chastened for our holiest thoughts, alas!
There is no reason found in all the creeds,
Why things are so, nor how it came to pass.

But in the heart of man a secret voice
There is, which cries, and will not be restrained,
Which says to grief: weep on, while I rejoice,
Trusting that somewhere all will be explained.

And again

It is no common failure, to have failed,
When man has given
His whole days labour to the task assailed,
Spent earth on heaven.

If error or if weakness enter here,
What helps repentance?
Remember this, oh Lord, in thy severe
Last sentence.

In short this poet possesses talents which might have
secred him a very high place among our modern writers, if
the had been properly applied; as it is, they have been
almst wasted in a struggle after effect. Yet we cannot
turn the leaves of Clytemnestra or the Wanderer without
lightng upon passages which, once read, can never be for-
gotte.

We cannot of course examine the works of the minor pets of our age. *Hood* deserves mention for his wit,
humor and tenderness. *Motherwell* the Scotch poet is re-
markole for his fine sense of beauty and the tenderness

and grace of many of his verses. His Jenny Morrison is one of the best poems our age has produced. *George Macdonald* occupies a middle position between our poets and novelists, but he belongs rather to the former than the latter class. His writings bear the impress of the German Romantic School, and they deserve particular attention for their grace, and the passionate fervour with which they teach the doctrines of forgiveness and self-renunciation, but we have not space to linger over them. The other poets of the day we must pass without mention.

CHAPTER III.

On turning to. the prose literature of our own age we must, before commencing our examination of the novels of this period, cast a glance at our essayists, as their influence has been widely felt by the greatest writers of that class. Foremost among these, both in originality and influence, stands *Thomas Carlyle.* His earliest works were a life of Schiller, and a translation of Wilhelm Meister. The first of these is remarkable as being one of the first attempts to introduce a really philosophical criticism into England. But it was little more than an attempt. The second is one of the best translations our literature has to boast of. In 1833 and 1834 Carlyle published Sartor Resartus in Fraser's magazine. This is a very extraordinary work. It purports to be the life and opinions of a German Professor; but it treats of almost every subject under the sun and of some things above it. As the life of the professor is the centre of the work, the point from which the thoughts spring, and round which they revolve, we will examine it first. The great doctrine on which the whole system of Carlyle is founded is that man does not live for pleasure (alone), else were our life of ne-

cessity wretched. „Will the whole Finance - ministers and
Upholsterers and Confectioners of modern Europe undertake,
in joint-stock-company, to make one shoe-black happy? „he
passionately exclaims". „ They can not accomplish it, above
an hour or two; for the shoe-black also has a soul quite other
than his stomach, and would require, if you consider it, for
his permanent satisfaction and saturation simply this allot-
ment, no more and no less: God's infinite universe
altogether to himself, therein to enjoy infinitely and
fill every wish as fast as it rose. Oceans of Hochheimer, a
throat like that of Ophiucus, speak not of them; to the infinite shoe - black they are as nothing. No sooner is your
ocean filled than he grumbles, it might have been of better
vintage. Try him with half of a Universe of an Omnipo-
tence, he sets to quarrelling with the proprietor of the other
half, and declares himself the most maltreated of men. — Always there is a black spot in our sunshine; it is even, as I
said, the Shadow of Ourselves". According to Carlyle it is
not pleasure but duty that is the chief end of man. But what
is duty? To bring oneself into connection with the laws of the
universe and to submit one's will to them, that is in his eyes
the great duty of each man. But how is this to be done in
our age of scepticism and insincerity? This is the question
which the life of the professor in Sartor Resartus is intended
to answer. In it the author endeavours to paint the various
phases of moral life through which a sincere and thinking
man in our age has to pass, before he can attain that belief in which he can find rest. The object of the tale has often been mistaken, and Carlyle has been blamed for not in-
dividualizing his hero, and for omitting, or passing lightly
over the externals of his life. But these did not concern him,
it was the soul with which he had to do. It was the human,
and not the personal part of our nature which he wished to
paint, that each man might find in the book a picture of himself. The rest of the book is taken up with remarks on things

in general, some of which display a strange, wild humour,
and others a still stranger pathos. The influence of German
thought may be traced in every page of this volume. It is
apparent in the very style, which is a strange mixture of ner-
veous and ideomatic English, and peculiar and mannerised
adaptations of German grammatical forms. All imitations of
his diction are disgusting, but it is well suited to his eccentric and fragmentary style of thought, and it often rises into
an eloquence which borders on poetry. The German philosopher to whom he is most indebted is Fichte, but, while
his thought wants the systematic development of that thinker,
his sympathies are broader and, I think, deeper. Some
passages of his writings seem to grasp and solve the riddles
which beset every thinking man in our days. Sartor Resartus immediately became a favourite of the most earnest of our young men. Its influence was similar in kind,
but much wider and deeper than that of Tennyson's „In
Memoriam“.

After the publication of this work Carlyle delivered several courses of lectures in London, and wrote essays for
several of our leading reviews and magazines. They treated principally German and French subjects, and exhibited
high critical powers, but it was perhaps the deep earnestness of their tone, and their wide tolerance that secured them
their vast popularity. In 1850 his Latter Day Pamphlets appeared. They treated the leading questions of the day. It
had always been Carlyle's motto, that it is our own faults
and the virtues of our neighbours that concern us, and in
these papers the faults of England are mercilessly exposed
and ridiculed. These pamphlets cost their writer many friends
and admirers. They had borne much general satire from
him, but they were enraged when he descended to particulars and laid bare the rottenness of the present state of
things. It is easy to join in a general confession that we
are miserable sinners, and to listen to a sermon upon cant

and hypocrisy, but when our favourite sins are denounced
and our own darling shams exposed, it is not so pleasant.
But the very fact that these papers excited so much uneasi-
ness proves that they were needed. When the patient shrieks
at the doctor's touch, we know that the part is diseased. Any
person who formed his estimate of England from these papers
alone would doubtless have a false idea of the country, yet
they are essentially true. Their great fault is the deification
of power, of mere brute force however used. This they share
with some of Carlyle's earlier, and most of his later works.
He does not believe with Napoleon that God is on the side
of the strongest battalion, but he seems to think that the
strongest battalion is generally on the side of God. It is
easy to see how he has come to this state of feeling. Gifted
himself with a deep and firm belief that sometimes almost
reminds us of the old Hebrew prophets, he moves among
the fine gentlemen and ladies of our modern literature like a
giant among pigmies. Your respectable gentleman is his
aversion. He has nothing in common with that agreeable
being, who is a master of small talk and shines in society, who has a pleasant little joke ready for every occasion and a sneer for any disagreeable truth, who is a faithful member of his party and keeps his eyes carefully shut
to any truth that transcends his little creed, who trips lightly
through the world, as if the universe were a colossal ball-
room, and there were no God enthroned above him, no
abysm gaping beneath him, who has no courage or heart to do
either right or wrong, who, as Dante says, is hateful alike to
God and to the enemies of God. His shallownes disgusts Carlyle,
and any reality, however rude, seems better to him than such
a sham. A great deal doubtless may be said on the other
side of the question, but a man must be judged by his own
belief, and if Carlyle be right, and God, as he bitterly says,
has not taken the devil into partnership, and the „Eat, drink
and take your ease" be not the highest of divine revelations,

then we can hardly wonder at the gloomy prophet's wrath and scorn. Since 1850 Carlyle has been engaged in historical works the best of which is the history of the French Revolution.

If we look at his general character as an essayist, which is what most nearly concerns us at present, we find, as I have already said, that much of his influence is owing to his deep earnestness. He never appeals to conventional laws or to the opinion of his age. He speaks, or at least he endeavours to speak, to something much deeper than the understanding, to what he himself calls, „the God-like that is in man." He endeavours to bring every question, be it literary, social or political, into connection with the noblest part of our nature. Hence the withering power of his sarcasm. We have agreed not to think too deeply on some questions, to be sharp and acute, but not really earnest about them, „to leave God and the soul out of the game", to admire mere cleverness, to be content with half truths. To this agreement Carlyle is a stranger. He speaks the truth most indiscreetly, and at the most unsuitable times. He places the highest standards before us, and in comparison with them the things we have admired look inexpressibly mean. When we have built up an exceedingly clever theory and defended it with logical acuteness against all common attacks, he comes and asks with the most intolerable earnestness, „Do you really believe it?"

A man who is thus in earnest has a vast advantage over those who appeal to lower standards. He gains a kind of moral influence over his readers, for we have naturally a respect for an earnest and sincere mind, and enthusiasts have always exercised a much wider influence than their intellectual power entitled them to. Hence the writings of Carlyle have done much to deepen and purify our modern literature. But what a man gains in depth by a firm belief, he generally loses in his range of sympathy. Enthusiasts are generally bigots. Their eyes are closed to every truth that lies

beyond their creed, their hearts have no sympathy for those
who do not belong to their party. Believing that the doctrines they teach are the truth, they cannot but think that
those who do not hold these doctrines are the enemies of the
truth. This is not the case with Carlyle. He has sympathy
for every great mind, whatever its belief may be. He can
admire Goethe and Mirabeau, Luther and Voltaire. No writer of the present day has a wider tolerance. This is proved
by his French Revolution, the greatest of his historical works.
He is not on the side of either party, nor does he even endeavour to put on the cold impartiality of a judge. He writes
the history dramatically. He identifies himself with each
party in turn. When he writes of the Mountain he is as de-
mocratic as Danton, when he speaks of the Queen he is the
most enthusiastic of royalists. It is instructive to compare the
manners of our three greatest modern historians, Buckle, Macaulay, and Carlyle. The first of these looks upon history
as a mass of raw materials, from which the great laws of national progress may be deduced. He cares little for the great
men who play a part in the senate or army, and nothing at
all for their private characters. It is with the spirit of the
age itself that he has to do, and all that can throw a light on
its character is interesting to him, be it a sermon, an anec-
dote, or a piece of scandal. The novels and dramas of a
country are more important in his eyes than its court and
royal marriages. Yet his aim is not merely to discover and
to portray the spirit of a period. He goes farther and shows
what influences assisted, and what retarded the advance of civilization, he writes rather the philosophy of history than
history. Macaulay and Carlyle, on the other hand, aim
simply at giving a picture of the age about which they
write. The latter, it is true, assures us in some introduc-
tory chapters, that the French revolution was Gods judgement on quacks and liars, but his purpose, like that of
Macaulay, is on the whole, rather to give a picture of the

time, than to deduce great laws from it.   Here however the
resemblance between the two ceases.   Macaulay gathers as
much information about his characters as he can get, he then
chooses the most salient parts of it, and gives them to the
reader.   He paints his characters with great skill, as Scott
did, from without inwards; and he is very careful to add
nothing that he cannot support by good authority.   He is not
troubled by apparent discrepancies in his characters as long
as they are historically proved.   He lets you see them as
nearly as possible as their contemporaries saw them, and pro-
nounces judgement upon them in almost the same tone as we
judge our every day acquaintances.   With what wonderful skill
he does all this, I need not say.   Carlyle pursues a very different
method. After carefully collecting every thing that can throw a
light on the person whose life he is describing, he endeavours to
form an idea of his character, and to reconstruct it as a poet
does.   He is not contented with giving us his words and
actions, he endeavours to lay bare the nature from which
those words and actions spring.   Sometimes he does this by
a clever nickname, and sometimes by long pages of description.   This is what gives his narrative the strong dramatic
interest which we find in no other historian.   We feel that
we have to do with men, and not with mere abstractions.
His history has the interest of a poem.   His Mirabeau and
Danton excite feelings akin to those which are touched by
Macbeth and Lear, rather than those which are awakened
by other historical portraits.   But there is a danger in this
style of writing.   When the mere facts are given us, we
can form what idea of a character we will, we can test it by
facts derived from external sources, and judge it for ourselves.   But with characters presented to us in Carlyle's manner this is impossible, we must accept them, or leave them.
If you take his picture as the true one, it is as impossible to
have two opinions on the moral worth of the character, as
to dispute over the crimes and virtues of Macbeth.   It is how-

ever but justice to add that most critics praise the truth of
Carlyle's pictures, and that the publication of papers which
were inaccessible to him has, it is said, almost invariably
supported his opinions.

, Lord *Macaulay's* essays possess many of the beauties of
his history. But few of them are purely critical. He uses
most of the books, whose names are placed above them, merely as texts from which he can diverge to any interesting
subject which falls in his way. Nor is the literary criticism
that is to be found in them very deep. Macaulay seldom
touches on the principles of art, or refers to the great laws
which govern literary composition. He is content to judge
separate cases, to detect unwary authors, who have stolen
stray-thoughts or indulged in bad Latin. He is decidedly
greater as an historian than as a critic.

Hallam is certainly a far greater critic than his more
brilliant rival, many would add and a greater historian, but
that is a question on which I can form no opinion. His
Introduction to the Literature of Europe in the 15th, 16th and
17th centuries is by far the greatest work on literary history in our language. It is of course impossible for me to
enter into an examination of the works of our critics and essayists. I should be but ill qualified for such an undertaking,
nor does it lie within the plan of this book which has to do
with our imaginative literature alone.

CHAPTER IV.

Polonius divided the plays of his day into tragedy, comedy, history, pastoral, pastoral comical, historical pastoral,
tragical historical, and tragical comical, and critics of his
disposition would find it easy to divide the novels of our age
into at least twice as many classes. A much more simple
classification will suffice for our purpose. Successful novels
may be divided into two great classes, those whose interest is
temporary, and those whose interest is permanent. To many
this would seem like dividing them simply into bad or good
tales, but this is not the case.   To write any successful book
a certain talent is needed, and a novel that runs through a
dozen editions in as many weeks can not be an entirely stu-
pid work, even though it should be forgotten at the end of
the year. Many such tales are written.   We can remember
many novels which we have read with breathless interest,
but which once finished we cast aside and never opened
again.   On examining these books we shall find that their
interest depended on one of two things. It was due either to
some external circumstance, or to the plot of the tale. When
a nation is interested in any subject, a novel putting the popular view of the matter into a startling light often has a success quite disproportioned to its literary value.   During the
Catholic reaction, for example, a tale dealing with the horrors of the inquisition, or having for its villain a crafty Jesuit
was almost sure to find a large circle of readers. The reason
of this is obvious.   The middle classes in England have a
strong instinctive hatred of Catholicism.   This had been
brought into play by the numbers of converts which had
passed from the Anglican to the Catholic church. They were
enraged, they knew not why, and any libel however absurd,
any falsehood however ridiculous, was gladly credited and
eagerly read.   As soon as the excitement had passed away,

the tales it had produced were forgotten. But by far the greater number of novels which have a great temporary success are those whose interest is centred not on external circumstances but on the mere plot. These are the books which we cannot lay down till we have finished them, and which, once finished, we never take up again. They treat of great crimes, strange adventures and striking events. We are interested in the fate of the heroes rather than in the heroes themselves. The tale excites curiosity that is almost feverish, but as soon as this curiosity is satisfied it has no farther hold upon us and is therefore never reread. The most successful novel of our age unites both kinds of temporary interest. Uncle Tom's Cabin is at once a very clever sensational story and a popular statement of the popular theory of slavery. Hence its vast success. In vain critics showed that the characters were impossible and the sentiments exaggerated and sickly, in vain thinkers protested that the arguments were one-sided and false. It passed from house to house, and from land to land. It was read by every one, it was discussed every where. Thackeray, Dickens and Hawthorne were forgotten. Who reads it now? Who will remember its name in fifty years time? Such must be the fate of all tales whose interest depends on the story told rather than the manner of telling it, on the material rather than the form. But the form must be taken in its widest sense, as embracing the characters, the wit, humour, and pathos of the tale, not the mere development of the plot, though the latter is a more important element in a good novel than some modern authors are willing to believe. — Of the first class of novels we have already said enough, they have no claim to be considered works of art. They may therefore interest the historian and the student of social life, they do not concern the literary critic.

Foremost among the novelists who belong to our second class, both in time and versatility, stands *Bulwer Lytton*. He has tried his hand at almost every kind of novel and, though few, if any, of his works can be said to belong to the highest rank, none of them are entirely unworthy of notice. His earlier works bear many traces of Byron's influence. Paul Clifford and Eugene Aram have some resemblance in tone to the writings of the Jung Deutschland school. Their heroes are criminals, and from their tone one would almost fancy that no person could be interesting who had not been guilty of felony at the very least. I endeavoured in my remarks on Byron to point out some of the reasons for this strange taste. In the works of Bulwer and his followers these influences may still be traced, but another and more important one came into play. In the writings of the middle ages a man is generally represented as either bad or good, and when he has once been placed in either of these classes no further explanation is thought necessary. It is the nature of a saint to be a saint, and of a villain to be a villain. What more need be said? Of course in the highest works of art which the middle ages produced there was something more than this. But the character of literature at that time was to motify as little as possible, to paint the devil very black and the saints very bright. Modern times have dealt very hardly both with the devil and the saints. We should doubtless have found some excuses for the first, had it not been easier to get rid of him altogether. Who would not rejoice at his departure? And, since he has gone, and the saints have no more work to do in the universe, they too have disappeared. We have discovered that good people are not so very good, nor bad people so very bad as our forefathers thought them. We have begun to suspect that our own natures contain the germs of the same passions which lead one man to the murderer's gallows and another to a martyr's stake. In short tolerance is one of the characteristics of our time. How nearly this virtue may be related to scepticism, does not concern us here. Whether we find so much good in the worst, so much evil in the best characters from Christian charity and humility, or merely because we have no very strong belief in either good or evil, is a question which we need not ask. It is enough that the tolerance exists, that we no longer draw a broad line between the good and the evil, but see in the worst and best of characters men and brothers. This being the case, it follows as a matter of course, that the change from good to evil must form an interesting subject for artistic treatment. In the Elizabethan age it was frequently treated. During the dominion of the French or classical school poetry became too shallow to grapple with such subjects, and we find few traces of crime. That is crime subjectively considered with reference to its effect on the criminal's character as a tragical subject during that period, unless we stretch the word so as to make it cover the sins of Richardson's heroes. When however our poetry was again freed from foreign influence, it was natural enough that it should recur to such subjects. It was not the material, but the manner of treating it that was unhealthy. This will at once be seen if we compare Macbeth with Eugene Aram. In both a murderer is the hero, in both he excites a lively and deep interest. In both he is represented as no inhuman monster, but as a man with like passions to ourselves. Where then lies the difference? In the treatment of the subject. With all our interest in and sympathy for Macbeth we never loose sight of his guilt. Shakespeare keeps clearly before our eyes the fact that murder is a fearful crime. Our feelings, even while they sympathise with the hero, condemn him. It is in this feeling that the moral influence of the work lies, far more than in the mere fact that at the end the hero is killed. We see a truly grand and noble character, led step by step to a deed which places him not, it is true, beyond the range of our sympathy, but at least in a position

12 *

which we shudder to think of, a position in which all that
is good in his character must needs be turned to evil. The
tragic power of the piece depends on the fact that crime is
crime. In Eugene Aram this is not the case, the hero becomes interesting because he is a murderer. The guilt is lost
sight of. His punishment is entirely external. No ghost
disturbs him. No horrible consciousness of crime haunts
him. He himself declares, he never knew remorse. His rest
is broken, it is true, but it is broken only by fear that punishment may overtake him. Still the novel is powerfully
written, and, though the tone is unhealthy, it is not immoral. Unfortunately men who had neither the talents nor the
sound moral sense of Bulwer imitated him in the choice of
subjects, and a series of criminal novels arose. These works
cannot be too severely censured. Their authors reason thus. A
good and great character may fall into crime; therefore there is
nothing so very bad in crime. Starting with the perfectly
correct belief that a criminal is not a monster but a human
being, and that the very feelings which might lead to the noblest virtues can, when misdirected, lead to the most fearful
sins, the writers of this school arrive at the strange conclusion
that there is after all no difference between vice and virtue,
good and evil. It is as if a physician should undertake to show
the progress of a physical disease, and the very influences
which in health strengthen and nourish may, when dis-
ordered, produce illness and death, but in the middle of
his dissertation he should become confused and should state
that these evil effects were after all signs of the most perfect health. The unhealthy moral tone is not however the
only fault to be found with these tales. Few of the writers
of this class have dared to provide no punishment for the
crime at last. In the end the hero is executed, and the
author exclaims, what more will you have, behold the punishment of murder. But in fact he has commited two faults

instead of one. His hero does not deserve to be executed.
If, as he has taught us, moral law does not exist, why pun-
ish this pure and noble being? If murder is only an amiable
weakness, why execute the murderer? He is unjustly
treated, and we are us deeply enraged with human as with
divine laws. This is the only effect that poetical justice can
possibly have in the hands of such writers. In his later
works Bulwer has entirely freed himself from this love of
moral paradox which in truth he never carried to such length
as his followers. „The Caxtons“, „My Novel“ and „What will
he do with it?“ take deservedly a high place in our novel literature. One characteristic of this author can hardly be
too highly praised. He never looks upon authorship as a
mere means of gaining fame or profit. Art is a sacred thing
to him. Hence, whatever the faults of his works may be, they
are free from levity and conscious a struggle after false effect.

Disraeli's novels are brilliant and full of wit and paradox. They abound in original social, religious, and philosophical theories. They bear witness to the learning, culture,
and mental power and dexterity of their author. No ordinary
man could have written Coningsby, or the Psychological
Romance. No one who was without the „fine fire of genius“ could have conceived and executed the character of Si-
donia, and no common character would have undertaken his
chivalrous defence of the Jews. His very errors are dazz-
ling and bear witness to the subtility and force of his intellect and the vigour of his imagination. But his tales can
scarcely be said to be true to nature, and it is fortunate both
for his country and his fame that he has devoted his brilliant
and various talents to the service of the state.

The works of *Anthony Trollope* occupy a higher place
than those of the above authors in execution, though not
in intention. He is not so ambitious as they in the choice of
subjects. He is content with simple domestic events, but

he treats them in a masterly manner.   His novels are char-
ming tales.   They realise the old idea of a novel better than
any works of the kind our age has produced.   They are
books which fill up a leisure-hour very pleasantly.   They
require no deep thought, they suggest no new and startling
views of life, they are what they profess to be, a recreation
and no more.   The characters are correctly drawn, the conversation is light and witty, the style has the elegant ease
of a gentleman's conversation.   No writer of the day is
equally successful in painting English respectable life.   Thackeray anatomizes it; Dickens distorts it into humourous con-
tortions; Trollope simply reproduces it.   All common forms
of character are familiar to him, and he paints their outside
well.   Sometimes he tries to do more, and he has once or
twice succeeded, but, as a rule, he is content to write
pleasant and graceful tales.   He pays more attention to
his plot than most novelists of our age have done, and his
stories are interesting, without having any of the unhealthy
and feverish excitement which belongs to the sensational
novel.

   Charles Dickens is the most widely popular writer our
age has produced.   The work on which his fame is founded
is the Pickwick Club.   It was published in 1837, in monthly
numbers, and had an unparalleled success.   As it is a good
example both of the beauties and faults of its author's writings,
we may enter into an examination of it.   It is a series of
sketches bound together by a very slight thread.   Four gentlemen, members of the Pickwick club, make a journey through
England to observe the manners of different classes of society.
The book is the story of their adventures   Nowhere in our
literature, except perhaps in the comedies of Ben Jonson, are
an equal number of comical situations to be found.   I know
of no other book over which one can laugh so heartily.   The
fertility of the author's imagination is truly marvellous.   The

characters are conceived and drawn with an appreciation of comical effect that cannot be overpraised, and with a knowledge of London life which, though it is far from being as exact as it appears, is still vast and varied. The diction is strikingly original, and proves that Dickens has a sharp ear for homourous stylistic effects. In his later works this has degenerated into mere mannerism and trickery, but in the Pickwick papers this was not the case, and there is something irresistably comic in the way in which he sometimes uses long rhetorical phrases for simple every-day objects. The situations too, improbable as they are, are worked out with such truth of detail, and so cleverly modified that they seem at the first glance not only probable, but real. But the Pickwick papers are far from being without faults. The most apparent, and perhaps the greatest of these is the love of horrors for their own sake which the author displays. This is the more inexcusable, as they form no necessary part of the plot and are only introduced as episodes, in the form of tales, by the different characters. We have one, for instance, describing the death of an actor in Delirium Tremens. Such a subject is merely disgusting and therefore entirely unfit for artistic treatment. In a great work it might possibly have been introduced as the necessary end of a long course of folly, but even then it must have been treated with great delicacy not to produce utter loathing. But here it is introduced for no apparent reason, with all its grotesque horror, into the midst of the humourous characters and comic adventures which form the staple of the book. The very realism and power with which it is painted makes it all the more hideous. It is idealised by no poetic touch, enobled by no redeeming trait, it is utterly loathsome. It produces a certain effect on the reader, no doubt, but it is no artistic effect. Horrors of all kinds are exciting, and they are for that reason degrading, unless they produce something more than mere excitement. If they produced no effect, the gladiatorial games of ancient Rome, and the Bull-fights of modern Spain would have had no demoralizing influence on those who witnessed them. Were mere excitement the end of art, an execution would be the most artistic of modern spectacles, for what tragedy can equal in horror such a sight? It is because Lear and Macbeth produce something more than mere horror that they are works of art. Dickens has not even the excuse of the great dramatists of the Elizabethan age. Many of them produced scenes at which we now shudder, but they did not cover the stage with racks and red hot irons merely to give the spectators the brutal excitement of watching a wretch's agony, but to show the power of the heroes soul and his steadfastness in the strongest possible light, and when reading their plays, we admire while we shudder, while we turn from Dickens's scenes of horror with simple disgust.

The characters of the Pickwick papers have, as I have said, a great appearance of reality. They are, like those of Scott, drawn entirely from the outside. But Dickens is far inferior to the earlier poet both in range and truth. There seems to be no end to the fertility of Scott's imagination. He can picture the highest and the lowest. The king on his throne and the beggar in his hovel, the old knight errant and the modern gipsy are equally familiar to him. Dickens rules over a much more limited kingdom. London low and middle-class life is his proper sphere. A farmer, it is true, and even an elderly lady living in the country he can paint with some power, but when he leaves such subjects he gets beyond his depth. Nothing can be more false and melodramatic than his scenes from high life and his historical novels. This is less apparent in the Pickwick papers than in his later writings, because they move in the society which he can depict most happily. But we find, when we turn to the Old Curiosity Shop, Oliver Twist, or indeed almost any of his longer tales, that he cannot paint the whole even of the limited world in which he is most successful. His works are a collection of oddities, and even these he cannot follow into all the phases of life. Scenes of humour and simple pathos like the death of a child he can draw with great power, but he can do little more. Deep passion he cannot even depict or describe, far less express. He always writes melodrama when he attempts it. His love-scenes are mawkish and sentimental in the extreme. He is equally unsuccessful in drawing criminals, though he generally introduces at least one into each of his stories. He is always careful to motify the externals of his tales, he seldom even attempts to .do this for his characters. Take Quilp, the most hideously grotesque of all his creations, a being, by the way, as impossible physically as morally, whose two great pleasures are drinking boiling brandy and tormenting everybody who comes in his way; as he stands he is a simple monstrosity. By what steps did he sink to that depth of evil? Shakespeare has drawn a Richard III and an Iago, but he has condescended to trace their downward way, to show us the influences that led them to their bad eminence; Dickens is satisfied when he has drawn a nightmare. But, even in the field in which he is most at home, the characters of Dickens are inferior to those of Scott. The latter writer, though he drew his characters from the outside, drew each as a whole. Dickens does not do this. He seizes upon one or two outward traits or habits, and patches them together into .a character. These habits are striking and generally taken from real life, so that they give a strong air of reality to the figure. But, if we look deeper, we too often find that there is nothing behind them. In his later novels this has gone so far that each of his comic characters has a phrase which he constantly repeats, and by which he is known, so

that a modern critic says, it would be easy to draw up a list
of his characters and their characteristic expressions.   In his
women characters he is particularly unfortunate.   Old ladies
and servant girls, it is true, lie within the range of his genius.   But his young ladies are all insipid and unnatural.
Florence in Dombey and Son, as soon as she ceases to be
a child, is a remarkable union of these two qualities.   Fancy
a rich and well educated young lady running away from home
and seeking a refuge with the father of her lover, a nearly
ruined shopkeeper, and an old and vulgar captain of the
merchant service.   And she is represented as a model of delicacy and virtue! His pictures of children, on the other
hand, are very beautiful.   Little Nell, Paul Dombey, and a
crowd of others are masterly in the extreme.   The fact seems
to be, that Dickens is a very exact and quick observer, with
a keen sense of humour, but without much feeling for grace
and beauty.   As far as his observation goes he has no equal;
whenever their is an opportunity for humour, he makes the
best of it.   But ugliness does not repel, indeed it sometimes seems to attract him.   For grace he seems to have no
sense.   His pictures all want delicacy.   This and a love for
striking situations are the causes of his greatest faults.

Another great fault of most of his novels is their want
of unity.   It would be unjust to blame the Pickwick Papers for this, for they are only intended to be a series of
scenes, but the same is the case with almost all his novels.
They are often discordant.   It would be difficult to find a
single one where the plot is harmoniously developed.   This
may be owing to the fact that they have all appeared in
monthly or weekly parts, with the exception of the smaller
tales.   Indeed, the works of Dickens are the most striking
example our literature exhibits both of the advantages and
disadvantages of periodical writing.   He is seldom or ever
dull.   One cannot read twenty pages in any of his works

without coming to some interesting scene. But there is something incongruous and discordant in most of his novels. Again, we find that, though the greater part of his tales are quietly and leisurely developed, they are almost all crowded towards the end, so as to leave the disagreeable impression that the author is in haste to get finished. Yet, after all, there are few pleasanter books than his novels. We return to them with pleasure ever and again. Pickwick never ceases to amuse and interest us. Their humour is proved by their immense popularity. In England every one reads them, and they have been translated into most European languages. I cannot of course enter into an examination of each of his works. The best among them seems to me to be David Copperfield. It contains, it is true, no scenes which equal in humour the best parts of some of his other tales, but the characters are better drawn, and the plot is much more probable and carefully constructed than in any of his other stories. This work too is much less mannerized than most of his are, and it contains passages which betray powers that we should not have supposed him to possess. In fact it makes us doubt if Dickens might not have become a far greater artist, had he attained a less general and early popularity. Perhaps much of its superiority lay in its form. It is an autobiography. Dickens is not, as we have seen, happy in drawing the depths of human nature, the internal character of his heroes. Even their outsides which he sketches so cleverly he usually tinges with a subjective feeling of fondness or dislike. This is a fault in a common novel, in an autobiography it is a beauty, for in it he has not to paint real people, but the impression such people make on the mind of his hero. We may doubt if the characters are quite possible as he represents them, above all we may suspect that behind the uncouth exteriors a human soul lies hid, a capability of love and sorrow, of tears and laughter, but we know that our impression of the people we meet every

day is one sided, and that we do not see into the depths of
their souls. Therefore we do not expect omniscience in David
Copperfield, and are not disappointed that the other characters
have sometimes rather scant justice at his hands. The later
novels of Dickens are far inferior to the earlier. The pathetic scenes are more melodramatic, the humourous scenes more
highly caricatured. Yet, with all his faults, Dickens is one
of our greatest novelists and by far the most popular of our
modern writers.

While Dickens was at the very summit of his fame, a
far greater writer, *William Makepeace Thackeray*, was slowly
fighting his way into public notice. He was known and respected by literary men long before the general public had
learnt to distinguish his papers from those of the other periodical writers of the day. Indeed he can hardly be said to
have become celebrated till 1847, when he published his
first great novel, Vanity Fair, in monthly parts. The plot
of this work is not very striking. Indeed Thakeray never
succeeds in interesting his readers in his tales. He seems to
look upon his incidents merely as a means of exhibiting his
characters. This is a fault, it is one of the things which
will always prevent him obtaining anything like the popularity of Dickens. One feels no feverish interest in his
stories, one lays them down without difficulty. Indeed one
does not care very much what the fate of Dobbin, Amilia
and Becky may be. But, if his books are easily laid down,
they are taken up again with pleasure and will bear rerea-
ding as few novels will.

One of their principal charms is the truth of the characters. The technic of Thackery in this respect is worthy
of notice. No writer of our age, except George Eliot, con-
ceives his characters so entirely from within as he. The whole
mechanism of their nature, their inmost thoughts and actions
are revealed to him. Yet he assumes an entirely outward
position, he talks about them as we do of real men and wo-

men. He pretends to guess at their feelings and motives. He says „It is only charitable to suppose so and so", but hints that there may be reasons for thinking otherwise. In fact he criticises them in the same way in which we criticise our friends and acquaintances as soon as their backs are turned and they are fairly out of hearing. This gives his characters a strong air of reality which is increased by his whole style of introducing them to us. At first we know little more about them than we do about the people we have met once or twice, that is to say we known their appearance, their position in life, and their style of conversation. In the course of time one little secret comes to light after another as if by chance, until at last they stand before us in their whole integrity. Thus in Pendennis it is not till Warrington is about to drop out of the story altogether, that we find the key to his character, his unfortunate marriage. To return to Vanity Fair. Foremost among the personages of this tale stands Becky Sharp, one of the best conceived and most exquisitely executed figures to be found in the whole range of English fiction. The daughter of a poor artist and a French dancing girl who dies shortly after her birth, she is educated almost exclusively among men. Her intellect which is naturally fine is excited and called forth in a thousand ways, while her heart is left untouched. The tenderness of a woman's care, the depth of a mother's love, those sweet remembrances of childhood which return reproachfully to the most hardened worldling and shame his selfishness, she never knew. She grows up in her father's studio, alternately coaxing away his duns and amusing his friends with her mimicry and wit. From hence she passes to the cold and dull respectability of a ladies' school. What could such a girl become, with what principle could she start in life but with that of utter selfishness? She adopts it deliberately and follows it consistantly. She looks at all other people as the mere means of her advancement and uses

them as tools.   She tries to gain their love that they may
help her, to make herself neccessary to them, that they may
serve her; when they are of no more use she casts them
aside.   If they oppose her she does not hate them.* Why
should she? It is a part of the game.   The vanity and affections of mankind she looks at in nearly the same light, they
are the weaknesses which put other people in her power.
There was still one hope for her.   Had she met a man of an
intellect equal to her own, who loved her deeply, a husband
in short, whom she could respect, she might have been
saved.   Instead of that she marries Rawdon Crawly, a man
who loves her passionately, it is true, but who has no intellectual power, who becomes her servant and no more.   Yet,
bad as Becky is, we never lose our interest in her; in fact,
we rather pity than condemn her.   She is rather unscrupu-
lous than wicked.   She never does wrong for the mere sake
of sinning.   There are too some slight but exquisitely true
touches which bring her within the reach of our affections.
Her short exclamation „If such a man had loved me so, a
man with a head as well as a heart, I should not have minded his large feet," moves me, I must confess, more than
all Amelia's sentimental troubles.   That young lady is the
exact opposite of Becky, a woman without any great intellectual power, quite an insignificant thing in fact, but a pure
and loving nature.   Every reader looks down upon her with
a feeling of sympathy not untinged by contempt.   Yet she
is an exquisitely finished character, and one that was probably much harder for the artist to draw than her more
brilliant rival.   Becky, once conceived, afforded by her
strongly marked character a firm point from which to proceed. It was easier to catch her likeness because her features
were more striking, while Amelia is one of those figures
which it is difficult to paint because they seem to have no individuality.   The faces which are the despair of portrait painters are not those which have a firmly marked form or a pe-

culiar expression, but those whose features have nothing remarkable about them, and whose expression is varied and
undefined. Such is Amelia, a simple, common-place, insignificant being enough, and just on that account a masterpiece. She and Becky are the two opposite poles of female
character, as it is to be seen in the drawing rooms of fashionable life — Thackeray's Vanity Fair. The male characters are just as masterly. The changeable, impressionable,
successful and superficial George Osborn is painted with wonderful truth. So is Major Dobbin, the awkward, faithful,
and really clever lover of Amelia.

The satire of the book deserves at least as much praise
as the characters. No satirist, since the time of Swift, had
displayed anything like the power of Thakeray, and the cy-
nicism of that great writer will prevent his books ever attain-
ing a wide popularity. Thackeray had much in common with
Swift. He had some of his powerful sarcasm, and in knowledge of men and their motives he is at least his equal. But
nothing was holy to Swift. Our best and our worst feelings
seem to him equally vain and foolish. He ridicules the love
of a mother to her children with nearly the same zest as the
follies of courtiers. His works are loveless and pitiless, we
shrink from them with something like dread. Thackeray on
the other hand, though he walks with a scornful smile among
the booths of Vanity Fair and decries the wares that are
sold there, has a heart full of tenderness. He is not sentimental, it is true, and I fear he can lay but small claim to
the charity that thinketh no evil. He has a little piece of
scandal to tell of most of the passers-by. He hints that the
jewels you are admiring are false, or hired for the occasion.
He whispers that the lovely lady who looks so gentle lays
her sweet temper aside with her fine clothes, and so on. But
his eyes brighten as he looks at the children, and his voice
grows soft as he tells you how their mother loves them, how
gentle she is, and what she bears for their sake. If you

chance to meet some poor wretch, at whom the world cries
shame, he does not join in the cry, but tells you, there are
excuses even for him, that he too has virtues of which
the world knows nothing, and that he might, had circumstances favoured him, have been very different. In short
Thackeray's tone always reminds one of Emerson's defini-
tion of Englishmen in general „He is a churl with a soft
place in his heart".

Vanity Fair was followed by Pendennis, a tale which
displayed all the powers that had made its predecessor popular, and which was written in a less bitter tone. The character of Miss Amory is equal to that of Becky Sharp both
in force and originality, and Warrington is perhaps the grandest character Thackeray ever attempted. A man of great mental powers and a strong will, he has been ruined by an un-
wise marriage with a girl of no education, and lives on, without hope or purpose, wasting his great genius on unworthy
objects. The character is developed with great power, and the
sketch is quite free of the sentimentality into which almost
every other writer of our age would have fallen, had he tried
his hand on such a subject. The death of Mrs Pendennis
is a scene of such true and simple pathos as it would be difficult to find anywhere but in the writings of Thackeray. His
customary bitterness makes his tenderness exquisitely touching. And Mrs Pendennis and Laura, pictures of pure and
simple womanhood, move through the tale with an indescribable purity and beauty. They seem to be Arthur's guardian
angels, and we cannot think that a man who is loved by
two such women can in the end be injured by the glittering emptiness of the society among which he lives. In this
work Thackeray aimed at something more than he had ever
tried before. He touched upon the intellectual side of our
nature, and in Arthur's character he has given a forcible
picture of the scepticism which haunts most young Englishmen. It is not a doubt as to this or that doctrine, or insti-

tution, but of all, a doubt as to the very basis on which all belief and action rests.

We cannot dwell at greater length on Thackeray's works. Each of them is a masterpiece in its way. He certainly excels Dickens both in truth to nature and power of satire. He is inferior to him in the production of comic situations alone, and, if humour be indeed „laughter with one's eyes full of tears", we must give him the higher place even as a humourist. Indeed it almost seems as if the absence of the purely comic element in his books is rather intentional than from want of power. There are passages and characters in his minor works, in the Shabby Genteel Story for example, which will bear a comparison with the best passages in Dickens's novels, even in comedy. But he saw that life is not made up of strange adventures, that nature does not delight in ludicrous monstrosities, however amusing they may be, and he was content to follow her teachings and paint things as they are. This is the reason that there is no self-repetition in his works and, that no mark of failing powers is to be found in the last them.

Dickens and Thackeray are usually classed together, and form with their followers what is called the London school of fiction. They treat as we have seen common every-day life, and they treat it realistically. All that part of English character which is to be found in the drawing-rooms of our aristocracy or in the beer-shops of the metropolis is open to them. They know the city too and can introduce their readers to merchant-princes and their clerks. They can introduce them into ball-rooms and betray the weaknesses of the ladies who move through them, and retell their love-tales. In short, all that makes up the worldly and domestic side of English character is their province; but farther they do not go. They know nothing of heroes and saints, and we must confess, London is not the most likely place to give birth to such characters. They do not paint enthusiasm. The self-

devotion of the priest, the scholar and the artist is incomprehensible to them.   They are all haunted by an uneasy
conviction that after all a pretty wife, a good position
in society and a large income are the chief ends of life.
The instinct which prompts some men to cast . all these
aside, that they may spend their lives in bringing hope and
peace to the cottages of the poor, that encourages patriots
to die on the scaffold for a principle that can bring them
no wordly good, that forces artists to give up riches,
position and comfort for the hope of creating some great
work, in short the whole demonic side of our nature is
a sealed book to them.   It appears in their works only as
folly or knavery.   But these feelings have not died out in
England, they have only taken the form which it is most
difficult for educated people who stand beyond its influence
to appreciate, a religious form.   It is impossible for any person, who examines impartially the religious phenomena of
our age, to doubt that amid the follies and incoherencies of
our sects there is something that is not foolish or incoherent,
some real self - devotion and earnestness, something that is
true to the highest part of our nature.   It is impossible to
deny that the forms of the Anglican church are something
more than a grand and beautiful ritual, that the spirit of that
church is a great power levening society, that it softens the
hearts of the rich, and opens up to the poor a realm of pure
· and holy thoughts which cast an ideal glory over the common cares and humble work of their every - day life.   With
these things the London school of fiction cannot deal.   It is
interesting to observe the different positions which Thackeray
and Dickens take up with respect to them.   Dickens simply
ignores all the feelings which are unworldly except when
speaking of very little children. He has some sympathy with
religion, it is true, when it takes the Christmas form of roast-
beef and plum-pudding, but anything that goes beyond these
seems hypocrisy to him.   Thackeray on the other hand

speaks with a certain awe of all holy things. Occasionally
a tone, as from a far country hinting at such subjects, is to
be found in his novels, as for example in the death of
Mrs Pendennis and Colonel Newcombe, but for the most part
he draws back from such subjects as from things unsuited to
the character of his tales.

But feelings which absorb so much of the attention of
Englishmen could not fail to be mirrored in our literature.
Thus we find that a great part of the novels of our day are
religious novels, and truly it would be difficult to find a
series of works which are as a rule more absurd, narrow
and inane than these. Their cant is only equalled by their
dullness. Their heroes are for the most part pale - faced cu-
rates of high birth and small means, who after three volumes of mental struggles die of a decline, deeply lamented
by the female part of their congregations. The tone of these
works is ascetic in the highest degree, but it is a gentlemanly asceticism which wears white surplices and unim-
peachable linen.

Muscular Christianity was a reaction against these absurdities. Its chief representative is *Charles Kingsley*, a
novelist of real power. Of all religious or critical theories that of the Muscular Christians seems to me the worst.
Carlyle's worship of brute force is bad, the bigotry and
narrowness of the religious novelists is at least equally
so, but to have united the evils of both systems seemed impossible until the genius of Mr Kingsley accom-
plished it. The heroes of his school must be at least
six feet high and must be able to drink unlimited quan-
tities of beer and smoke incredible numbers of cigars.
They must be able to hunt and box, and these talents
must be exercised in the course of the tale. Still they
must be religious men, strict members of the church of
England, who during the intervals of their more active du-
ties can fall back upon religious enthusiasm and internal

13 *

conflicts with evil. In short the highest characters these writers can conceive are hunting bishops and praying prize-fighters. Their villains are equally strange and original. They are not dark and cruel men, nor intriguing lawyers, nor desperate thieves, for all these have energy; and power, be it used for good or ill, is the god these writers worship, the one virtue they respect. Their villains are men of re-finement and polish, who delight in art and have weakness enough to shrink from fighting with bargemen and to know very little about horses and to care very little for hunting.' For Chatterton dying in his garret, for Shelley living a life of long continued martyrdom for what he believed was true and right, the Muscular Christians have no sympathy. They never speak of Goethe without a sneer, and the trait in our Saviour's character for which they have the greatest sympathy is the fact that he „came eating and drinking". In short, spite the talents of some of its supporters, Muscular Christianity seems to me one of the most unhealthy signs of our modern literature. It tends to foster the worst vices of our national character, our insular self-deifying patriotism, our bigotry and our utili-tarianism — vices which the greatest minds England has produced in the last hundred years have done their best to combat or to satirize.

Still, several authors of this school are men of real ta-lent; among these we have only space to notice Charles Kingsley. Within certain bounds his power of drawing character is doubtless great, but his genius is continually hampered by his theory. Thus one always feels inclined to side against the author in judging his characters. He seems to have a personal hatred to some of them and a most unjust partiality for others. It is strange that after drawing both the author should never have perceived, that John Briggs whom he is perpetually abusing and who is killed off at the end of the work, is a far nobler character than his brutal favourite Tom Thurnall who rewards the girl that saves him from drowning at the risk of her life by accusing her of theft, and persecutes a man who never did him an injury under pretence of improving his treatment of his wife. In short, Kingsley has no tolerance for differences of character, a quality which is by the bye much rarer than tolerance for differences of opinion and much more necessary for an artist. Even the latter he does not possess in any great degree. His bigoted hatred of the nonconformists peeps out every now and then in the most comical spite. Grace's mother is an excellent specimen of this. She is a methodist and a thief. Now, had Kingsley worked out this character, had he shown her internal life, had he revealed the outbursts of her emotional religion and traced their influence in weakening her moral nature, he might have drawn a very powerful picture, or at least have created a character that had an internal reality and necessity. This he does not even attempt. She is merely a lay figure, a part of the machinery of the tale and nothing more. Why then make her a methodist?

These flaws in his works are the necessary results of his principles. Where they leave him free to follow his genius, he develops great artistic power. Hypathia and Westward Ho! are novels of a high order, and the many beauties of Two Years Ago more than outweigh its faults. In it the genial character of the author every now and then comes to light in spite of his Muscular Christianity, as in the character of Claude Mellot, the artist who according to the usage of the school ought to have been executed at the conclusion as an idler instead of being dismissed with honour. His writings too have always a manly tone and he is not afraid of describing the world as it really is. In a word his faults are those of his school, his beauties are all his own.

CHAPTER V.

In 1859 the literary world of London was astonished
by the appearance of Adam Bede, by *George Eliot*. It was
at once evident to all thinking people that this novelist must
be placed among the very greatest of our writers, that
Thackeray alone, if even he, could be placed as high. The
work run through five editions in as many months, yet it had
nothing sensational about it. It was a simple tale of every-
day English life. Everybody was busied with guesses as to
the real name of the author. We will content ourselves
with the published name and speak of the writer as George
Eliot, spite the current and probably correct report that
this gentleman is after all no gentleman, but a lady.
Adam Bede was not the author's first work. In 1858
he had published three novelettes under the title of Scenes
in Clerical Life. This work had passed almost unnoticed
at the time, yet it is a very remarkable book. The
three stories treat three thoroughly different sides of human
life. The first, the position of a man in society and his
money-difficulties; the second, passion; the third, moral
life. Each tale displayed very extraordinary power and a
knowledge of human nature as exact as it was varied.

Yet this book was inferior to Adam Bede. The tales
had not nearly the same interest as tales, and they had
not nearly the same range. Of the book taken as a whole
this cannot perhaps be said. The three great moments
of human life were treated in it, but they were treated
separately. This is a fault into which many novelists fall.
They look at the world from a single point of view, they
consider it merely in its relationship to a single set of interests. Thus their pictures seem exaggerated and distorted.
For the universe is not a church, nor a ball room, nor a
workshop, it contains all these and many things beside. A

man may be a good Christian, but, if he is worth anything,
he will not always be on his knees; he may be a faithful
lover, but, if he is in a healthy state of mind, he will not
spend his whole life in writing sonnets to his lady's eye-
brow; he may be an earnest worker, but, if he is anything better than a machine, other thoughts will intrude on
the work he has in hand, he will devote some of his time
to interests that lie outside his workshop or his studio. It
is one of the great advantages of the novel, that it leaves the author room to draw a full man, to show the different sides of his character, to paint his various and often dissimilar interests. This is not equally the case with
the drama. In it only a single moment in a man's life can
be taken, the great crisis of his fate. This crisis is often, nay
generally, brought about by a single set of feelings gaining the
entire mastery over him. In Macbeth it is ambition, in Romeo
and Juliet love, which hurries the hero on to his destruction.
This set of feelings must be painted with as much force as
possible, in order that the hero's fall may be motified. This
is one of the great difficulties on which dramatic authors suffer ship-wreck. Some paint only the set of passions necessary for the piece, in which case we have stage-heroes instead of men, others paint the whole characters with so great
exactness that the dramatic element is lost. It is only a
great master like Shakspeare who can hint at other sides of
the hero's nature than those which hurry on the catastrophe,
without bringing them into undue prominence. In the novel
this difficulty does not exist. The novelist is not obliged
to crowd his whole story into a piece that must not occupy
more than three hours in acting, he is not obliged to force
all he has to say into a series of striking situations. He has
therefore more room to paint our many-sided life. If he does
not do this, he neglects one of the greatest advantages of the
style of writing he has chosen. In treating great and simple
catastrophes the novel will never equal the drama. In de-

lineating those wild bursts of passion which seize a man
and hurry him on, as if against his' will, to crime or destruction prose can never equal poetry. It is because such situations and catastrophes as are suited for the drama are unusual, because our life is not made up of wild bursts of un-
governable passion, that the prose novel is a neccessary
form of art. It is because in our age dramatic subjects are
rarer than ever, and such passion is almost incredible, that
now the novel is the most popular of all artistic forms. Of
all English novelists George Eliot has comprehended the purpose and scope of the novel best. In Adam Bede almost
every feeling which could enter into the sphere of life in
which the tale plays is touched upon. Love plays a great
part in it, but it is no mere love-story; religious sentiments
and feelings are touched upon, but it is no religious novel;
there are scenes of humour in it, far superior to anything
Dickens ever wrote, but the interest is not centred upon
them alone. This is not equally the case with the Scenes
in Clerical Life; still they are masterly stories, far the
best novelettes in our language.

Adam Bede is a tale of English country-life. It begins in
the year 1799 and ends in 1807. That was the time when the
Evangelical or Low church party was gradually fighting its
way upwards in the church, and Methodism was gradually
spreading among the lower classes. The hero of the book, Adam
Bede, is a carpenter. He is a man who delights in his work
for its own sake, but is not without the English wish to
get on in the world. He is a cunning workman and has
that kind of practical intellect which helps a man to do his
work, whatever it may be, well. He has no taste for the
doctrinal subtilties in which his brother Seth delights and
but little liking for his emotional religiousness. He thinks
there is such a thing as being over spiritual, that a man
needs something besides the gospel to be able to build coal-
pit engines and Arkwright mills. „But to hear those

preachers, he exclaims, you'd think that a man must be
doing nothing all his life but shutting his eyes and looking
what's going on inside him. I know a man must have the
love of God in his soul, and that the Bible's God's word, but
what does the Bible say? Why it says that God put his spirit into the workman that built the tabernacle, to make him
do all the carved work and things that wanted a nice hand".
Adam has a firm will and clear idea of what is right and
honourable. This makes him sometimes rather hard to
others. It is not easy for him to forgive. He does not bear
his father's drunkeness or his old mother's querulousness
with nearly as much patience as his brother Seth. He does
his best to keep things in order at home, but he can't
help saying an angry word now and then. A very characteristic trait in his character is conservatism. On building and wood work he has an opinion of his own, and
he is willing to support it. He wishes to see all the new
inventions introduced into his neighbourhood as quickly
as possible, but he is not anxious for any farther change.
He „can't bear a fellow who thinks he makes himself fine
by being impudent to his betters". Yet Adam is not a
cold moralist, he can love and hate as the story proves.
When he is wronged even unintentionally, he has a fierce
thirst for revenge which neither Seth nor Arthur Donnithorne can understand. He is one of those men who cannot sit still under injustice or sorrow. The very energy
of his nature makes him long to do something, if it is only
to find a vent for his feelings. He is in short an exact
picture of the better kind of peasant artisan. His brother,
Seth, has a strong family resemblance to him, but he is inferior to him both in intellect and force of character. He is
a Methodist. Much of his intellectual power is spent on religious discussion. His temper and pride have been quieted
down by religious emotions. He reads biographies and
theological books while his brother is studying mathematics.

His very love for Dinah, deep as it is, has little of the
stormy selfishness of passion. It too is tinged by his emotional
religion. He is more patient, forbearing and gentle than
Adam. He gives up Dinah to him almost without a struggle.
While Adam's power is centred in himself, Seth seeks something external to lead and guide him. He leans on Adam,
he asks counsel of Dinah. His religion is a staff which supports him. In difficulty Adam would be apt to go over both
sides of the question by himself and form his judgement
alone, Seth would probably go to some friend for advice,
or take the first text that struck him as a mysterious guidance.

Strongly contrasted with both these young men is Arthur Donnithorne, the heir to the squire. He is rich and
well educated, high spirited and noble minded. Everybody likes him, and he wishes well to everybody. He is
kind and affable, always ready to do a kindnesss to any one.
He is determined, when he becomes squire, to be a model
landlord and set a good example to all the people round.
But then his goodness is all impulse. He has no firm
principle, he does right because it pleases him to do so.
When wrong things seem pleasant, he does not cast them
away from him as Adam would, or pray himself out of a desire for them, as Seth would, he looks longingly at them,
and argues with himself about them, and resolves not to do
them, and does them. The struggle in his mind about Hetty
is powerfully and delicately depicted, more delicately than
anything of the kind which I remember in our whole novel-
literature. He makes a half appointment to meet her and
resolves not to go. He rides away to get out of temptation
and comes back in time to keep his appointment. He is angry with himself and determines never to see her again,
and then thinks she may suppose, he is in love with her, and
get wild fancies into her head, so it will be better to go and
undeceive her. He goes, but forgets the reason of his going

as soon as he sees her. Then he goes to breakfast with
Mr Irvine, the clergyman, that he may tell him all about it,
and comes back without doing so.

Adam always looks the future fairly in the face, and
calculates cooly the chances for and against him. Seth
takes no thought for the morrow. Arthur always hopes for
the best and puts disagreeable chances out of sight and
trusts to his luck. We must now turn to the women.

First comes Hetty. It is very difficult to describe her.
She is very pretty, very vain and very shallow. Her character is not at all beautiful, it wants depth and simplicity,
it is utterly selfish. She takes no interest in the children
that grow up around her and partly under her care. She
does not hate them, but she thinks them troublesome, quite
uninteresting things. She has no love for her uncle and
aunt who bring her up at their own expense. Even her
love for Arthur is not true, self-forgetting passion. More
than half of it is vanity. She is pleased that a gentleman
loves her. She thinks that her love must end in a nice house,
fine clothes and no work. Yet the impression of her beauty
takes such a hold on the reader, that he, like Arthur and
Adam, is almost in love with her faults.

Dinah is as exact a contrast to Hetty as can well be imagined. She too is beautiful, but her beauty does not leave
an impression on the mind as that of her cousin does. It
is chastened down and subdued by the beauty of her mind.
She is a methodist and works in a factory. This is never for
a moment lost sight of. She is not witty nor clever nor well
educated. Yet she influences all who see her. The roughest
are respectful to her. The least considerate drop their
voices when they speak to her. It is her spiritual life, a life
of long continued self-devotion, which gives her this charm.
She does not ask herself what is pleasant, but what can I do
to be of use to others, where can I be of the most use? She
always lives as if in the presence of a higher power. She

looks upon her duty as the work God has given her to do.
She goes to him for help, comfort and guidance. Hence
beneath her simple, Methodist phraseology a deep meaning,
lies hid. We may look upon her as the incarnate ideal
of Methodism in its first and purest period. There is no
other writer of our age who could have painted such a
picture of a spiritual life. Our admiration for it and the
genius of the author is heightened when we turn to the
character of Mr Irvine, the clergyman of the town. He is
a perfect gentleman both by birth and education, but with
comparatively small means. He lives unmarried that he may
keep his mother and sisters in the ease and luxury to which
they are entitled by birth. He is loved by the whole of his
congregation, for he is a good-natured, open-hearted man.
His tenderness to his delicate sister and his affection for his
mother are exquisite traits in his character. But he is no
saint. He does not like Dinah feel that his life is but a
charge from God. The whole world is not to him a temple.
His every act is not a prayer. He is indolent, fond of chess,
of horses and of dogs. He loves the classics more than the
fathers of the church and „finds a savouriness in a quotation
from Sophocles and Theocritus that is quite absent from any
text in Isaiah or Amos". His very tolerance smacks of indifference. He is so kind to Dinah because after all he is
not so very much in earnest for the doctrines of the church.
His sermons were short moral essays, not doctrinal discourses
or deep inquiries into Christian experience. Yet I must confess he is a great favourite of mine, the character in the
whole book whom I like best. Mrs Poyser too is perfect in
her way. She is a good bustling farmer's wife, with a sharp
tongue and a sharper wit, a woman with a tender heart,
but one who keeps every thing in order and loves to rule.
Many of her speeches have the true ring of old proverbs.
We may take an example or two. She says of Craik, the
Scotch gardner, „he's like the cock who thought the sun got

up to hear him crow", and again „if you could make pudding
with thinking of the batter, it would be easy getting dinner. —
Those who choose a soft for a wife may as well buy up the
short horns. — If you get your head stuck in a bog, your legs
may as well go after it". Of Dinah she says, „It comes over
you sometimes as if she'd a way of knowing the rights of
things more than other folks have, but I'll never give in, that's
because she's a methodist, no more than a white calf's white
because it eats out of the same bucket as a black one". — „You
make but a poor trap to catch luck, if you go and bait it with
wickedness".

I might go on talking about these characters and others
in the book but it would be useless to do so. They are
all drawn to the life and, what is more, so arranged that
the principal characters stand out clearly and the others are
subordinated to them. They are, too, dramatically developed. That is to say we find out their characters from their
words and actions, not from long descriptions, and when we
close the book, we feel as if we were taking leave of old
friends.

But psychological truth is not the only, or perhaps even
the chief merit of Adam Bede. As a story it is exceedingly
interesting. No sensational novel could excite so lively an
interest as Hetty's flight awakens. The very shallowness and
weakness of the poor girl's mind excite our pity, as the sorrows of a child might do. We feel she is but ill qualified to
bear the passion and despair which surround her on every
side. It is this disproportion between her character and her
fate which makes the story so pathetic.

The influence of the German literature and particularly
of Goethe's writings is clearly to be traced in Adam Bede.
But it is no mere imitation like that in which other English
authors have so frequently indulged, it is real study. The
scene in the grove for example has much of that indescribable charm which attaches to Goethe's love-scenes, and which,

as far as I know, is to be found nowhere in our literature
but in the novels of George Eliot.   Yet there is no scene
in all Goethe's writings in which circumstances at all similar
are treated.   It is the spirit, not the mere accidents which is
imitated.   But the author has studied nature much more closely than any writer.   Every page bears witness to a most
exact and close observation of men.

    We must pass over the Mill on the Floss without any
notice at all except the remark that neither here nor in
any other book of the author is there any trace of self-repetition.   Silas Marner too must not detain us long.   This is, of
all the novels I know, the one in which the interest is most
purely intellectual.   We are not excited by the story.   Our
interest is concentrated on the development of the hero's
character.   As a study of character it is exceedingly powerful,
as a novel it is inferior to Adam Bede both in interest and
variety.

    In Romola George Eliot entered a new field.   His
name was so intimately connected with English country-life
that it was with a general feeling of surprise that English readers heard that the author intended to write an historical novel.
The age in which the story plays is one of marked contrasts.
The scene is Florence, the place where these contrasts were most
glaring.   It is the age of Lorenzo di Medici, of Macchiavelli, of
Savonarola.   On one side we have the heathen epicureanism and
refinement of the scholars of that age, on the other the deep
faith of the reformer.   Here we have the high endeavour
and great success of the artist, there the daring enterprise
of the merchant and the deep intrigue of the politician.   The
scene is bright and varied, the characters are strange and
striking.   This age George Eliot has conjured up before us.
Every side of that varied life is introduced into the tale.   The
scholar, the politician, the artist and the monk, each play
their part in the story, and to each justice is done.   It is
hard to divide the characters into groups because they are

not as in most novels contrasted by pairs, each is, so to speak, contrasted with all the rest. Thus Savonarola may be said to be the exact opposite of Tito, but he is equally opposed to Bardo, to Piero di Cosimo, to Dolfo Spini, and even to Nello.

We have not space to analyze the various characters, but we must linger, a few moments, over the three, most prominent. First among these stands Tito, the beautiful, clever and subtle hero of the novel. He is a man of a pleasant, sensuous nature, of great and well cultivated talents. Like all men of a highly wrought and delicately balanced constitution, he shrinks from pain. He has positively no principles, but he has a firm will and a clear intellect. He loves the applause, wealth and pleasure, particularly those intellectual pleasures which wealth alone can furnish. He is in short a character which can become either good or bad as circumstances may decide. During the whole tale we see his fall, a gradual descent from innocence which was not virtue to treachery and infamy. Evil is not pleasant to him, but he is driven into it step by step. He does not like deceit, treachery and cruelty, but he likes scorn and poverty still less. He is the personification of intellect and emotion, without conscience or passion. This character is delineated with masterly truth and skill. It is too a character which could only be produced by the circumstances and age in which he is placed, in the land and time of Machiavelli.

Savonarola's is a very different character, it is perhaps the greatest which any English author has attempted to draw since the age of Shakspeare. He is at the beginning of the tale a pure and sincere enthusiast. He endeavours to become, in thought and deed, a true Christian. From the depth of his heart he speaks to the people words of fire that go directly to their hearts. He speaks of justice and mercy, and they rush to hear him. But he feels that neither the church nor the state are what they should be. He uses his in-

fluence to bring about reform. For the same end he endeavours to increase his influence. But, to gain and retain his
hold on the minds of the people, he is obliged to lower his
ideal. At last, when five enemies of his party are unjustly
condemned to death and a word of his would save them, he
is silent. Outwardly he rises ever higher, internally he
sinks ever lower. His rapt devotion, and his noble simplicity have given place to ambition and a somewhat tortuous
policy. His ambition is, it is true, still noble, but it is not
entirely free from egotism. He will reform the church, he will
regenerate the world, and then he will lead the united hosts
of Christendom against the Turk and the Saracen. It is not
till the power has passed from his hands, till his dreams have
been wrecked, and he has learnt to say. „I am not worthy
to be a martyr. The truth shall prosper, but not by me"
that the faith and purity of his early days return to him.
Such is a sketch of Savonarola, as he appears in Romola.
He is the grandest character in the tale, perhaps in any modern English tale, and yét, in this character, the greatest
fault of the work seems to me to lie. It is finely conceived
and, the critics say, that it is historically correct. The author has evidently endeavoured to make it so. But there is
something that is of more importance in a work of art than
correctness, and that is clearness. An historian may have
doubts about his various characters; he may say, this and
that seems to be irreconcilable, but there is proof of both,
or he may say, this view seems probable, but it cannot be
proved. The poet has not this right. He must create his
characters. He may add to what history says about them,
and he may take from it. But his characters must be clearly
drawn, and must not admit of a doubt. Let us take an example. The fact that both Elizabeth and Mary Queen of
Scotts were vastly different in reality to the characters which
Schiller drew of them does not in the least affect the poet-

ical value of Marie Stuart. If new records should come
to light which made it clear that Macbeth and Richard III
were spotless characters, Shakespeare's dramas would not
lose any of their importance by the fact. Thus, when
George Eliot had once chosen Savonarola as a character, she should have drawn the picture fully and left us
without a doubt. The historian may find it difficult to recon-
cile the accounts of the last days of that ill-fated reformer,
he may with justice say that the official statement is so
garbled that it is impossible to get at the truth. The novelist should not have done this. He should have led us to
the cell, where he passed through his last mental struggles,
and have shown us the great soul bowed down by its anguish,
as he showed it exalted by high hopes and vain dreams.
As it is we have a clear picture of his mind down to the time
when he is imprisoned, and after that we are left in doubt.
This seems to me to be the great, the one fault of the book.
There were difficulties certainly to be overcome in doing this.
The torture was perhaps the greatest of these, as it would
have been impossible to show us the reformer on the rack,
which certainly had an influence upon him.

Romola's character is finely conceived and well developed, though perhaps its last phases are passed rather lightly over. In her the polish of the heathen and the earnest self-resignation of the Christian elements of the age are
united into something higher than either could alone produce.

When we turn from the other novelists of our age to
the works of George Eliot, we feel at once that we are enter-
ing a new realm. The difference is not quantitive, it is qual-
itive. It is not that his novels are merely better than those
of Dickens and Thackeray, they are something utterly different and indefinitely higher. The first peculiarity of his
style is its realism, its simple truth to nature. Like Wordsworth he can say,

The common growth of mother earth
Suffices me — her tears, her mirth,
Her humblest mirth and tears.

It is this love of and truth to nature, which has preserved George Eliot from the greatest faults of our other novelists. His characters have nothing odd and eccentric about
them, they are simple and natural, real studies from nature.
If we compare Adam Bede with Sam Weller for example,
this at once becomes evident. The one character is clever,
amusing, and false, the other is real and interesting on that
account. In fact the difference between George Eliot and
Dickens is the same in character as that between Shakspeare and Congreve, though of course it is far less in degree.
The one strives after effect, he dazzles by a blaze of wit.
Every thing his characters say or do is comic or pathetic in
the highest degree. The other aims at truth. With a wit
at least as brilliant and a humour of far vaster grasp, he is
content to bridle these, and to give them their proper place as
ornaments alone. Therefore there is hardly any trace of external comic in his writings. If we compare a passage of the
Pickwick papers, say the scene in the garden of the ladies-
school with the conversation of Mrs Poyser and Bartle Mas-
sey in Adam Bede, the difference of the two manners becomes at once apparent. The comic of the first scene depends
entirely upon the situation. To be found at midnight in the
garden of an establisment for young ladies, is a strange position for an elderly gentleman of strictly respectable habits.
The appearance of such a gentleman, in torn clothes and
high excitement, before an elderly and highly fastidious lady
in curl papers has something incongruous about it, which
provokes a smile that has nothing at all to do with the characters of the people concerned. Nor do their characters con-
tribute in the least to the details of the scene. These details
are taken from nature, but they are generalized and not individualized. The spinster lady of the establishment, the

three teachers, the five female servants, and the thirty boarders do not act as individuals but as representatives of a class. Upon this a great part of the humour depends. The rest is owing simply to <u>verbal trickery</u>. In the scene from Adam Bede on the other hand the humour depends entirely on the characters of the disputants. Each word gives us a glance into the secrets of the two characters, and it is this which makes the scene so humourous. This is what I mean in saying that the humour of Dickens is external and that of George Eliot organic.

This brings us to the second great difference between this writer and the other novelists of our age. He is not only realistic in his treatment and choice of subjects, he is also idealistic, indeed he is the greatest idealistic writer of our time. To say that an artist is at once idealistic and realistic may seem like a contradiction in terms. And so it would be, if I used the words in one sense. The word idealism, as applied to art, is so undefined that it may be well to explain what is meant by it here. In every person there are certain qualities which seem to be necessary to his individuality, and others which are purely accidental. These latter, in the real world around us, often overhang and hide the others, so that we can seldom see the real man through the mask that hides him. For example a man of real refinement and a cultivated taste may squint. This is something purely accidental, a defect that has nothing to do with the essence of his character. These accidental circumstances the idealistic artist omits, and thus the true character is brought to light. This we call artistic idealisation when speaking of poetry. Now George Eliot is the only writer of our age who can be said to do this, Dickens's characters are for the most part drawn in exactly the opposite way. They are <u>made up of accidents</u> alone. Every great poet idealizes, and the greatest, such as Shakespeare and Goethe, do it most. One cannot point to a single trait in Othello, Macbeth, Hamlet,

14 *

Faust or Egmont, which is not characteristic. We know
why Othello is black and Richard III a hump-back, that
is to say, we can trace the effect of these circumstances
on their characters. Just so there is nothing superfluous in
any character in Romola or Adam Bede. Every part of
each character has on organic relation to every other part.
This is evidently not opposed to realism of treatment. In
George Eliot the two manners are united, as they are in a
higher degree in Shakspeare and Goethe. The tone of the
novels we have been examining is as different from that of
other novels of the day as can well be imagined. They have
the gay and healthy objectivity of genius, a tone equally opposed to flippancy, melancholy and dogmatism. The author's
mind seems to have no whims and crotchets. He is content to let his characters play their parts, without using
them to teach either a moral or an immoral lesson. This is
a rarer quality than it at first seems. Most poets have theories to which they cramp their characters. What are Childe
Harold, the Giaour and the Corsair but the means by which
Byron teaches a false and unhealthy theory? But few, like
the author of Adam Bede, are content with a purely artistic
purpose. This is one of the reasons why his tales remind
us rather of the breezy freshness of the fields and woods,
than the close and unhealthy air of a study or a theatre.
Yet his novels have a far higher moral value than those of
any of his contemporaries, just as the plays of Shakespeare
are more moral, in the true sense of the word, than the
best story for little girls and boys. He does not teach that
mere external happiness is the end of life. Indeed none of
his novels end very happily. Yet they satisfy us. The happiness of his heroes is rather internal than external They
reach a height, from which they can look down on the
changes of the world. This too is the result of his truth to nature. Is not the great French woman right when she says,
that the theatre is the only place in our world, where vice

is punished and virtue rewarded? Is it not true that the most virtuous men are not the most successful, that those who lead the purest and noblest lives are not those who gain what the world thinks the highest prizes in the great lottery? If this is the truth, and who can doubt it, why should we create a false system of rewards and punishments in our novels? Why are we there to shut our eyes persistently to the fact that the good things of life, its pleasures and enjoyments, are not meted out, like an old nurse divides her sweet-meats, according to the merits of the receivers? It is not better openly to state the fact, as George Eliot does, that this is not the case, and that just for that reason pleasure is not the highest good, nor pain the greatest evil; that we are not like children to do good only that we may get a store of sugar-plums, either in this world or the next, or to avoid evil for fear of the cane or the black man that hides in the nursery chimney, but rather, because good is good and evil evil, to choose the one and avoid the other? That this is healthy morality in practice, can scarcely be doubted; and that these principles may be applied to poetry, the grandest tragedies of Germany and England prove. George Eliot has shown that they are at least equally applicable to the novel. Yet there is nothing ascetic in his writings. He does not turn with a puritanical scowl from the cakes and ale, or deny that ginger is hot in the mouth. His characters do not despise the good things of this life any more than sensible men in reality do, on the contrary they confess that pleasure is pleasant, that riches and comfort are good things which it is worth while to pay a high price for. They do not prefer water to wine, or sack-cloth and ashes to silk and fine linen any more than we do. But the best characters in his novels, like the best men in the real world, do not make these things the one or even the principal end of their life. Nor does he pretend to reward the sage and the martyr with a coach and four and a sufficient income, as if these were

a sovereign balm for all the ills of life. This is owing partly
to his truth to nature, and partly to the spirit of his tales, in
which, as I have said, all the various sides of human life are
mirrored, to the fact that his heroes have minds and souls as
well as hearts.   But we must pause.   George Eliot is in my
opinion the greatest English novelist, the greatest writer that
England has in our age produced.   With him we will close
our sketch of the English novels of our period.   It has been
very imperfect.   Several important names as for instance
those of Currer Bell and the author of Paul Ferrol I have
passed over entirely without mention, and others I have
treated very slightly. My excuse is that a thorough criticism
of the novels of our age which deserve attention would alone
fill a much larger book than the present.

CHAPTER VI.

As we have now come to the end of our period, it may
not be amiss to cast a hurried glance at the ground over
which we have passed.   The period which extends from the
Restoration to the middle of the last century was, as we have
seen, a prosaic age.   It was the time of common sense, wit
and logic; not of passion, heroism and poetry.   It was a
useful and necessary phase in the development of our civilization, but not grand or beautiful one.   The history of our
modern literature is the history of a great revolution in the
thoughts and feelings of men.   This change was felt all over
Europe, in France and Germany even more than in England.
It was caused, as it seems to me, by two great impulses:
The first of these was idealistic, the second realistic.   The
first was a reassertion of that part of man's nature which had
been lost sight of by the philosophers of the seventeenth century.   It was not confined to literature, nor did it begin·

there. In France Rousseau taught a system of policy which, with all its superficial appearance of logic, was as beautiful and as unreal as a dream. It was a protest against the authority of the past, a declaration that the human race is „the heir of an infinite possibility". Hence, under the title of a „State of Nature", he held up to the admiration and for the imitation of his countrymen a social condition which, as he himself confessed, „exists no longer, perhaps never did exist, and probably never will." The words he spoke went directly to the hearts of his countrymen. They touched on chords which his predecessors had ignored; they awakened powers which had long lain dormant, and before the end of the century we find France engaged in the revolution — the most colossal endeavour to realize an impossible ideal which is to be found in the history of mankind. In Germany Kant commenced a revolution in thought which, if it was less noisy, was scarcely less important than that which had begun beyond the Rhine. He was succeeded by followers who were worthy of him, by men who once more raised philosophy to the place it had long ceased to occupy. The part that England played in this great movement was far less important than that of France and Germany, but we shall be totally unable to appreciate the changes which our poetry has undergone during this time, if we do not remember that it is but a moment in a great European change. The idealistic movement showed itself in our poetry by an endeavour to free the imagination from the laws with which the critics had hampered it. Once more our poets tried their hands on grand and irregular subjects. They ventured to express deep passion and to create beauty for beauty's sake alone. Didactic poetry was thrust into the background and at last entirely abandoned. Narrative and lyrical poetry took its place, and the spirit and forms of both ceased to be conventional and artificial. The old models were abandoned, and in their place nature was held up as the only true and in-

disputable authority.   Hence the realistic was the necessary
consequence of the idealistic movement.   Nature, it is true, was
often misrepresented, yet, when once it was allowed that it
was the highest model, it followed as a matter of course that
it would be studied.   Connected with these two impulses and
inferior to them was the influence of our earlier literature, or
perhaps we should rather say it was the form in which these
two influences worked upon the poetry of England.   The
idealistic-realistic movement took three forms, of which
the three works that we examined in our first and second
chapters may be looked upon as types.   The first of these was
principally idealistic.   The poets who belonged to this school
loved the heroic and the gigantic.   Finding but few subjects
in their own age to suit them, they led their readers into
distant lands and times.   They told of wild adventures and
titanic passion.   Their favourite heroes were knights and
robbers.   This school may be said to have opened with Percy's Reliques and to have reached its greatest height in the
works of Byron and Scott.   The second school inclined to a
kind of subjective realism.   They endeavoured to paint nature as they really saw it, and to state their real thoughts
and feelings upon it.   They avoided superlatives.   They did
not delight in deep passion or wild adventure; they chose
their subjects from modern every-day life.   The fault to which
the inferior writers of the first school were most addicted was
rant, that into which those of the second most easily fell
was common-place.   The third school is that of Chatterton,
Shelley and Keats.   These poets were as dissatisfied with the
common life of every day as those of the first school, but
they led their readers into a purely imaginary land.   Like
Spenser, their great model, they took hints from nature,
but they used them only as hints.   Their landscapes have
the gorgeousness, grace and unreality of dreams.   Nor did
they endeavour, like Scott and Byron, to paint heroism and
passion.   It is beauty, a strangely spiritualized and unearthly

beauty, which forms the subject matter of their verses. Hence we see that the character of the English literature of the first part of our century was caused by a reaction against that of the eighteenth. It is true that neither the idealism nor the realism of the age was entirely healthy; there is something exaggerated in the passion of Byron and the nature-worship of Wordsworth; Shelley and Coleridge were too dreamy ever to take a place among the greatest poets, and even in Scott we find too often a love for the unusual and improbable. The greatest poets of the day had not learned the truth of Goethe's saying „Here or nowhere is America", and those who had learnt this forgot that nature is not poetry, but the material from which poetry may be formed.

Another unhealthy sign was the struggle after a petty originality. Poetry was divided into cliques, each of which had its dialect and its manner. Each poet had his peculiar defects which he valued more than the beauties of his verses; they were the signs of his originality, and originality was genius. Hence our poetry was in this period mannerized in the highest degree. This too was a necessary effect of the reaction. One of the most noble characteristics of the age of Voltaire was its endeavour after universality. It showed itself in almost every field. In politics petty patriotism gave way before an enlightened cosmopolitanism. The channel, the Rhine, and the Alps were no longer looked upon as barriers beyond which no human sympathy must extend. Voltaire flattered England, Englishmen reverenced France. Even while war was raging between the two countries, the scholars and poets of both rose above a national jealousy and declared that they were first men and then Frenchmen or Englishmen. Never since the Reformation had the scholars and poets of different European countries stood in so friendly a relationship. In Science the same endeavour after universality is clearly to be seen in the hatred of onesidedness which the greatest men of the age exhibited. They were

sometimes shallow, it is true, but they were never narrow.
Take Voltaire for example. He was a poet, a satirist, a
dramatist, a critic, an historian and a philosophical essayist.
He had studied chemistry, mathematics, natural philosophy
and almost all of the natural sciences, besides being acquainted with the literature of most European nations, and well
read in the memoirs and travels in which his age was so rich.
Nor is he a solitary instance. Diderot was probably superior
even to Voltaire in the variety of his studies; and many
others were to be found who were scarcely less deeply read
than these.   In literature the same endeavour after universality is distinctly, though not so distinctly, visible. The
poems of Germany, Italy and England lost a great part of
their national typus.   There was an attempt on all sides to
reduce the poetry of different countries to the same standard,
and to do away with the individuality of the poet as far as
possible. But this was not all, the same influence made itself
felt in various and peculiar ways.   One of the strangest of
these was Diderot's theory of typical art.   According to that
critic a great reformation might be wrought in poetry if, instead of painting individuals, the poet were to paint types;
that is to say that, instead of representing John Brown a
person with a distinct individuality, who is by trade a shoemaker, he should paint shoemakers in general, or rather all
the peculiarities of shoemakers united in a single character.
This would be subversive of the very spirit of art. John
Brown can never interest us because he is a shoemaker,
but because he is a man, because he too can love and hate,
laugh and weep.   He confined his theory to comedy, it is
true, but even there it would be injurious.   The reaction, of
which I have already spoken, went almost as far in the opposite direction.   We have seen that it led our poets into
mannerism, it induced them too to choose very extraordinary
subjects and characters.   Before individuality in the poet had
been looked upon with anything but favour, now it was con-

sidered the highest beauty; formerly the poets had been told that they must only paint types, now they considered only oddities and monstrosities worthy of their attention.

· Such was the state of our literature during the first thirty years of our century. After the death of Scott a great gap exists in the series of our poets. Wordsworth, it is true, still lived and wrote, but of all the great poets who had surrounded him only Coleridge still survived, and he had almost left off writing poetry. Among our living poets a few still imitate or even exaggerate the peculiarities of their predecessors, but the greatest among them endeavour to fuse the schools into one, to unite the beauties of all or at least of several of the forms of poetry which were in vogue at the commencement of our century. This is more evident in the novel than in any other branch of our literature, as is natural, since it is the channel into which the greater part of our literary talent has flowed. Here too we find at the beginning of our period a division into schools and an exaggerated mannerism which is gradually giving way before a simpler and a purer taste. When examining Dickens's works, we found that his characters were only a collection of oddities, that the natural and simple forms of life were not highly flavoured enough to suit his taste. Even in Thackeray we found a certain one-sidedness. We saw that his genius was confined to a certain sphere of life, which he never even attempted to pass. When we look at the minor novelists, we find the same fault. Currer Bell, with all her talent never drew a man, and her heroines, interesting as they are, belong to a single and not very healthy class of women. They are all sensitive, energetic and self-conscious. Whenever she attempts to delineate the internal life of another kind of woman, she fails. Yet she is perhaps the greatest representative of the subjective, if not of the idealistic school. Her power of describing emotion and analyzing mental conditions cannot be too highly praised. Yet she is one - sided. But, when we come to

15 *

George Eliot, we find the two schools united, as they always
are in writers of the highest genius. His tales are more realistic than those of Dickens and Thackeray. Every incident,
every sentence bears witness to the closest study of nature,
and to a power of observation that far surpasses even that of
Wordsworth. But this realism is only the dress of the highest ideality. Nowhere in our literature since the close of
the Elizabethan age do we find characters so truly ideal in
the best sense of the word, as those in Adam Bede and Romola. Besides this they are natural. There is nothing eccentric or odd about them, nothing one-sided in the author's
treatment of them. We cannot yet say if the works of George
Eliot are the fitting close to the great series of the English
novelists of the nineteenth century, or the commencement of
a series far deeper and truer than that which is passing away.

E r r a t a.

page		for:		read:	
page	20	for:	Pope	read:	Dryden
-	51	-	devide	-	divide
-	53	-	mas	-	was
-	53	-	imense	-	immense
-	59	-	their	-	there
-	70	-	dispair	-	despair
-	80	-	Child	-	Childe
-	85	-	good husband and father	-	good husband if not a good father
-	105	-	I was throwing	-	'Twas throwing
-	107	-	We wept	-	He wept
-	128	-	Jone	-	Ione
-	131	-	whe	-	we
-	135	-	luxurient	-	luxuriant
-	143	-	heroes	-	hero's

Printed by Fr. Frommann.